Big Data
Analytics

Dr. Arvind Sathi

MC Press Online, LLC
Boise, ID 83703

Big Data Analytics:
Disruptive Technologies for Changing the Game
Dr. Arvind Sathi

First Edition
First Printing — October 2012
Second Printing — October 2013
© 2012 IBM Corporation. All rights reserved.

MC Press offers excellent discounts on this book when ordered in quantity for bulk purchases or special sales.

Corporate Offices:
MC Press Online, LLC
3695 W. Quail Heights Court
Boise, ID 83703-3861 USA
www.mc-store.com

Sales and Customer Service:
service@mcpressonline.com
(208) 629-7275 ext. 500

ISBN: 978-1-58347-380-1

About the Author

Dr. Arvind Sathi is the World Wide Communication Sector architect for the Information Agenda team at IBM®. Dr. Sathi received his Ph.D. in Business Administration from Carnegie Mellon University and worked under Nobel Prize winner Dr. Herbert A. Simon. Dr. Sathi is a seasoned professional with more than 20 years of leadership in Information Management architecture and delivery. His primary focus has been in creating visions and roadmaps for Advanced Analytics at leading IBM clients in telecommunications, media and entertainment, and energy and utilities organizations worldwide. He has conducted a number of workshops on Big Data assessment and roadmap development.

Prior to joining IBM, Dr. Sathi was the pioneer in developing knowledge-based solutions for CRM at Carnegie Group. At BearingPoint, he led the development of Enterprise Integration, MDM, and Operations Support Systems/ Business Support Systems (OSS/BSS) solutions for the communications market and also developed horizontal solutions for communications, financial services, and public services. At IBM, Dr. Sathi has led several Information Management programs in MDM, data security, business intelligence, and related areas and has provided architecture oversight to IBM's strategic accounts. He has also delivered a number of workshops and presentations at industry conferences on technical subjects including MDM and data architecture, and he holds two patents in data masking. His first book, *Customer Experience Analytics*, was released by MC Press in October 2011. Dr. Sathi has also been a contributing author in a number of Data Governance books written by Sunil Soares.

In memory of Professor Herbert Simon,
who sparked my curiosity in qualitative reasoning

To Neena, Kinji, Kevin, and Conal
for giving me the time, the encouragement, and the support in writing this book

Acknowledgements

First and foremost, I would like to acknowledge the hard work from the Information Agenda community in creating a world-class reference material. I have heavily referenced the material here, including the Business Maturity Model, the Solution Architecture framework, and a number of case studies. I would like to acknowledge Bob Keseley, Wayne Jensen, and Mick Fullwood for conceiving the ideas and organizing the reference material. I would like to acknowledge Tim Davis for his encouragement and for providing financial services examples. Jeff Jonas provided me with inspiration for experimenting with the ideas and provided me with much of the backbone for this book. The technical ideas were created with help from Beth Brownhill, Paul Christensen, Elizabeth Dial, Ram Dorairaj, Tommy Eunice, Rich Harken, Eberhard Hechler, Bob Johnston, Noman Mohammed, Peter Harrison, Daryl BC Peh, Steve Rigo, and Barry Rosen. The Dallas Global Solutions Center team—Christian Loza, Tom Slade, Mathews Thomas, and Janki Vora—provided valuable experimentations on the ideas. Mehul Shah, Emeline Tjan, Livio Ventura, Wolfgang Bosch, Steve Trigg, Don Bahash, and Jessica White have provided valuable business value analysis components in this book. I would also like to thank the Communication Sector Industry Consulting team—Ken Kralick, Dirk Michelsen, Tushar Mehta, Richard Lanahan, Rick Flamand, Linda Moss, and David Buck—for providing the opportunities, customers, and contributions to the Big Data Analytics solutions.

Next, I would like to acknowledge the excellent work from the IBM Business Analytics and Optimization consulting team. In particular, Adam Gersting, Joseph Baird, Anu Jain, Bruce Weiss, Aparna Betigeri, and John Held provided the ideas behind the business scenarios and use cases through their consulting activities. I would also like to thank Mark Holste for collaborations and brainstorms on these solutions.

The IBM Software Group product teams provided the much-needed case studies and product examples. I would like to thank Roger Rea, Dan Debrunner, and Vibhor Kumar for their help on the InfoSphere® Streams® product; Arun Manoharan and Patrick Welsh for their support in getting Vivisimo® information; Andrew Colby for help on the Netezza™ Analytics Engine; Shankar Venkataraman, Girish Venkatachaliah, and Karthik Hariharan for Big Insights®; Claudio Zancani for Optim™ Privacy; and Mike Zucker for SPSS®.

I worked closely with the practitioners as I studied Big Data business opportunities. This includes Anthony Behan, Ash Kanagat, Audrey Laird,

Bob Weiss, Christine Twiford, Carmen Allen, Dave Dunmire, Doug Humfries, Duane Gabor, Gautam Shah, Girish Varma, Harpinder Singh Madan, Harsch Bhatnagar, Jay Praturi, Jessica Shah, Jim Hicks, Joshua Koran, Judith List, Kedrick Brown, Ken Babb, Lindsey Pardun, Mahesh Dalvi, Maureen Little, Neil Isford, Norbert Herman, Oliver Birch, Perry McDonald, Philip Smolin, Piyush Sarwal, Ravi Kothari, Randy George, Raquel Katigbak, Richa Pandey, Rob Smith, Robert Segat, Sam King, Sankar Virdhagriswaran, Sara Philpott, Steve Cohen, Steve Teitzel, Sumit Chowdhury, Sumit Singh, Teresa Jacobs, Umadevi Reddy, Vasco Queiros, Vikas Pathuri, Von McConnell and Yoel Arditi. I am grateful for the insightful discussions and implementations in understanding business opportunities as well as current Big Data practices.

I would like to thank Cheryl Daugherty for her review of the book and Sunil Soares for inspiring me to write the book. Gaurav Deshpande did a fair amount of work behind the scenes to help me organize and fund the book. It was also Gaurav's inspiration to introduce the cartoon strip, which was eventually co-authored between the two of us. Susan Visser provided valuable help organizing the publication process. Katie Tipton provided valuable publication and editorial guidance.

Last, but not least, I would like to thank my wife Neena, my daughter Kinji, my son-in-law Kevin, and my son Conal for their inspiration, support, and editorial help.

Preface to the Second Printing

I would like to thank the readers of the first printing of *Big Data Analytics* for their very valuable feedback. The book provided good support for selling the Big Data Analytics concept to a nontechnical audience. For those of you who are interested in more technical topics, a number of books and articles are available now. For example, the technical details behind the use cases described in the book are now offered as a series of articles in IBM® developerWorks®.[1] In addition, IBM Big Data has a good library of videos that detail some of the use cases mentioned in sections 3.5 and 3.6.[2] The first printing was well received, and the need for a second printing is the most important endorsement of this book.

While it has been only a year since the initial printing, it seems a lot longer in this ever-changing Big Data marketplace. Big Data usage is expanding across many industries and organizations. Many of the use cases mentioned in the book are getting implemented and are demonstrating their potential for disruptive business change.[3] Among the communications service providers (CSPs), we have seen a maturing of attitude toward data privacy. AT&T's latest announcement is a positive sign that CSPs have a good understanding of the privacy issues and are able to establish a balanced policy that provides customers with better services while protecting their identity data from being misused.[4]

The open-source community has fueled the much-needed innovation in technologies. A number of established players, including IBM, are providing support to the open-source communities while enhancing open-sourced products with additional value-added accelerators and applications. These market forces are commoditizing the Big Data Analytics tools. A number of products and services are targeted toward industry-specific use cases and applications. The business value lies in these integrated solutions that combine tools to provide value-added services.[5]

In addition to the business-facing use cases (for examples, see Chapter 3), the IT community is exploring a number of horizontal use cases that are common across IT organizations. These explorations are important steps from IT organizations in increasing their awareness and understanding of the underlying technologies. Many of these use cases are targeted toward structured data in the traditional business intelligence infrastructures. The three most common use cases are summarized here.

Data warehouse augmentation. Many IT organizations are facing an ever-increasing data warehouse infrastructure and are interested in exploring Big Data Analytics for augmenting the data warehouse. Some of the augmentation is in optimizing the data warehouse to enable new types of analysis. Big Data technologies can be used to set up a staging area or landing zone for new data before determining what data should be moved to the data warehouse. Infrequently accessed or aged data can be offloaded from warehouse and application databases using information integration software and tools.

Big Data tables to replace SQL. Organizations often used SQL databases for data storage and retrieval, even in situations where most SQL capabilities were not needed. A number of batch operations required sequential file access with limited indexing. Technologies such as HBASE and Cassandra are providing opportunities to replace SQL with less expensive tools that offer the same performance at lower cost.

Improved visualization and discovery. Many Big Data technologies originally designed for unstructured data are equally suitable for structured data. Visualization and discovery of data in large data warehouses has been a challenge. As organizations pool more warehouse data into a "data lake," visualization and discovery of this data has similar requirements to what Big Data tools have been doing with large data sets in unstructured public data.

While exploring these use cases, it is important to conduct experiments where the data exhibits one or more of the 4 V's (Volume, Velocity, Variety, and Veracity) described in Chapter 1. The new set of tools offers significant performance and cost improvement, but it shines much better in the presence of high velocity and high volume. Big Data Analytics requires new skills and new approaches. IT organizations are finding ways to retool their environment. These use cases are an important conduit to adopting these tools on familiar ground.

I look forward to your exploration of Big Data Analytics and hope this book helps you in your endeavors.

Arvind Sathi
October 2013

Notes

1. Arvind Sathi, Mathews Thomas, Jinesh Radadia, Ken Kralick, and Richard Lanahan, "Explore the Advanced Analytics Platform, Part 1: Support Your Business Requirements Using Big Data and Advanced Analytics," IBM developerWorks, *http://www.ibm.com/developerworks/library/ba-adv-analytics-platform1/index.html*.

2. "Big Data, Big Opportunities for Communications Service Providers," IBM Big Data and Analytics, *http://www.youtube.com/watch?v=FIUFYyz03u8*.

3. For the Sprint case study, see *http://www.youtube.com/watch?v=eg8KSLAZ2HM*. For the XO case study, see *http://www.youtube.com/watch?v=-KOn0Qn0lgA*.

4. "Our Updated Privacy Policy," AT&T Public Policy Blog, *http://www.attpublicpolicy.com/privacy/our-updated-privacy-policy-2*.

5. *http://www.thenowfactory.com*.

Foreword

by Bob Keseley

We are seeing an unprecedented interest in Big Data Analytics around the globe. Top performers have declared themselves "Analytics driven" organizations. Savvy business and IT leaders are starting to leverage Big Data Analytics to drive substantial enhancements in their business models, partnerships, and business processes. While almost everyone is talking about Big Data at the tool or product level, successful organizations are focused on Big Data use cases and techniques that drive the greatest business value. They are focused on the "business" of Big Data Analytics. Arvind has taken the same perspective in *Big Data Analytics: Disruptive Technologies for Changing the Game.*

Over the past three years, our Information Agenda team has worked extensively helping organizations shape their Big Data Analytics strategies and solutions. Starting with the business is fundamental to the success of any organization. I am pleased to see a book starting with the business as the primary focus and exploring best practices across sales, marketing, customer service, and risk management, before linking them to the solutions and architectures that make it all possible. We hope you enjoy this book about evolving best practices and their impact on the competitive landscape. May it facilitate the right dialogue between your business and IT leaders.

Bob Keseley
Vice President, WW Information Agenda
IBM Software Group

Foreword

by Jeff Jonas

This book covers a number of Big Data use cases, architecture considerations, and the rise of emerging observation spaces (social, geospatial, etc.) and covers some of the thorny issues around data privacy. An organization's available observation space (data they can get their hands on within law and policy) is growing faster than their ability to make sense of it. As organizations struggle to keep up, they are being forced to reconsider what kind of infrastructure will be required to harness Big Data.

Going forward, organizations must be able to sense and respond to transactions happening now and must be able to deeply reflect over what has been observed—this deep reflection is a necessary activity to discover relevant weak signal and emerging patterns. Following fairly recent experiments involving how humans piece jigsaw puzzles together, I have witnessed the criticality of tightly coupling discovery from deep reflection right back into the real-time sense and respond analytics. In fact, as the feedback loop gets faster and tighter, it significantly enhances the discovery.

The organizations that figure out how to make sense of what they learn fast enough to do something about it while it is happening will be more competitive.

Jeff Jonas
IBM Fellow and Chief Scientist
IBM Entity Analytics

Contents

Big Data Analytics:

Disruptive Technologies
for Changing the Game

By Gaurav Deshpande & Arvind Sathi

Chapter 1
Introduction

Big Data Analytics is a popular topic. While everyone has heard stories of new Silicon Valley valuation bubbles and critical shortages of data scientists, there are an equal number of concerns: Will it take away my current investment in Business Intelligence or replace my organization? How do I integrate my Data Warehouse and Business Intelligence with Big Data? How do I get started, so I can show some results? What are the skills required? What happens to data governance? How do we deal with data privacy?

Over the past 9 to 12 months, I have conducted many workshops with practitioners in this field. I am always fascinated with the two views that so often clash in the same room—the bright-eyed explorers ready to share their data and the worriers identifying ways this can lead to trouble. A similar divide exists among consumers. As in any new field, implementation of Big Data requires a delicate balance between the two views and a robust architecture that can accommodate divergent concerns.

Unlike many other Big Data Analytics blogs and books that cover the basics and technological underpinnings, this book takes a practitioner's viewpoint. It identifies the use cases for Big Data Analytics, its engineering components, and how Big Data is integrated with business processes and systems. In doing so, it respects the large investments in Data Warehouse and Business Intelligence and shows both evolutionary and revolutionary—as well as hybrid—ways of moving forward to the brave new world of Big Data. It deliberates on serious topics of data privacy and corporate governance and how we must take care in the implementation of Big Data programs to safeguard our data, our customers' privacy, and our products.

So, what is Big Data? There are two common sources of data grouped under the banner of Big Data. First, we have a fair amount of data within the corporation that, thanks to automation and access, is increasingly shared. This includes emails, mainframe logs, blogs, Adobe PDF documents, business process events, and any other structured, unstructured, or semi-structured data available inside the organization. Second, we are seeing a lot more data outside the organization— some available publicly free of cost, some based on paid subscription, and the rest available selectively for specific business partners or customers. This includes information available on social media sites, product literature freely distributed by competitors, corporate customers' organization hierarchies, helpful hints available from third parties, and customer complaints posted on regulatory sites.

Many organizations are trying to incentivize customers to create new data. For example, Foursquare (*www.foursquare.com*) encourages me to document my visits to a set of businesses advertised through Foursquare. It provides me with points for each visit and rewards me with the "Mayor" title if I am the most frequent visitor to a specific business location. For example, every time I visit Tokyo Joe's—my favorite nearby sushi place—I let Foursquare know about my visit and collect award points. Presumably, Foursquare, Tokyo Joe's, and all the competing sushi restaurants can use this information to attract my attention at the next meal opportunity.

Sunil Soares has identified five types of Big Data: web and social media, machine-to-machine (M2M), big transaction data, biometrics, and human generated.[1] Here are some examples of Big Data that I will use in this book:

- Social media text
- Cell phone locations
- Channel click information from set-top box
- Web browsing and search
- Product manuals
- Communications network events
- Call detail records (CDRs)
- Radio Frequency Identification (RFID) tags
- Maps
- Traffic patterns
- Weather data
- Mainframe logs

Why is Big Data different from any other data that we have dealt with in the past? There are "four V's" that characterize this data: Volume, Velocity, Variety, and Veracity. Some analysts have added other V's to this list, but for the purpose of this book, I will focus on the four V's described here.

1.1 Volume

Most organizations were already struggling with the increasing size of their databases as the Big Data tsunami hit the data stores. According to *Fortune* magazine, we created 5 exabytes of digital data in recorded time until 2003. In 2011, the same amount of data was created in two days. By 2013, that time period is expected to shrink to just 10 minutes.[2]

A decade ago, organizations typically counted their data storage for analytics infrastructure in terabytes. They have now graduated to applications requiring storage in petabytes. This data is straining the analytics infrastructure in a number of industries. For a communications service provider (CSP) with 100 million customers, the daily location data could amount to about 50 terabytes, which, if stored for 100 days, would occupy about 5 petabytes. In my discussions with one cable company, I learned that they discard most of their network data at the end of the day because they lack the capacity to store it. However, regulators have asked most CSPs and cable operators to store call detail records and associated usage data. For a 100-million-subscriber CSP, the CDRs could easily exceed 5 billion records a day. As of 2010, AT&T had 193 trillion CDRs in its database.[3]

1.2 Velocity

There are two aspects to velocity, one representing the throughput of data and the other representing latency. Let us start with throughput, which represents the data moving in the pipes. The amount of global mobile data is growing at a 78 percent compounded growth rate and is expected to reach 10.8 exabytes per month in 2016[4] as consumers share more pictures and videos. To analyze this data, the corporate analytics infrastructure is seeking bigger pipes and massively parallel processing.

Latency is the other measure of velocity. Analytics used to be a "store and report" environment where reporting typically contained data as of yester-day—popularly represented as "D-1." Now, the analytics is increasingly being embedded in business processes using data-in-motion with reduced latency. For example, Turn (*www.turn.com*) is conducting its analytics in 10 milliseconds to place advertisements in online advertising platforms.[5]

1.3 Variety

In the 1990s, as Data Warehouse technology was rapidly introduced, the initial push was to create meta-models to represent all the data in one standard format.

The data was compiled from a variety of sources and transformed using ETL (*E*xtract, *T*ransform, *L*oad) or ELT (*E*xtract the data and *L*oad it in the warehouse, then *T*ransform it inside the warehouse). The basic premise was narrow variety and structured content. Big Data has significantly expanded our horizons, enabled by new data integration and analytics technologies. A number of call center analytics solutions are seeking analysis of call center conversations and their correlation with emails, trouble tickets, and social media blogs. The source data includes unstructured text, sound, and video in addition to structured data. A number of applications are gathering data from emails, documents, or blogs. For example, Slice provides order analytics for online orders (see *www.slice.com* for details). Its raw data comes from parsing emails and looking for information from a variety of organizations—airline tickets, online bookstore purchases, music download receipts, city parking tickets, or anything you can purchase and pay for that hits your email. How do we normalize this information into a product catalog and analyze purchases?

Another example of enabling technology is IBM's InfoSphere Streams platform, which has dealt with a variety of sources for real-time analytics and decision making, including medical instruments for neonatal analysis, seismic data, CDRs, network events, RFID tags, traffic patterns, weather data, mainframe logs, voice in many languages, and video.

1.4 Veracity

Unlike carefully governed internal data, most Big Data comes from sources outside our control and therefore suffers from significant correctness or accuracy problems. Veracity represents both the credibility of the data source as well as the suitability of the data for the target audience.

Let us start with source credibility. If an organization were to collect product information from third parties and offer it to their contact center employees to support customer queries, the data would have to be screened for source accuracy and credibility. Otherwise, the contact centers could end up recommending competitive offers that might marginalize offerings and reduce revenue opportunities. A lot of social media responses to campaigns could be coming from a small number of disgruntled past employees or persons employed by competition to post negative comments. For example, we assume that "like" on a product signifies satisfied customers. What if the "like" was placed by a third party?[6]

We must also think about audience suitability and how much truth can be shared with a specific audience. The veracity of data created within an organization can be assumed to be at least well intentioned. However, some of the internal data may not be available for wider communication. For example, if customer service has provided inputs to engineering on product shortcomings as seen at the customer touch points, this data should be shared selectively, on a need-to-know basis. Other data may be shared only with customers who have valid contracts or other prerequisites.

Over the past year, the Information Agenda team has been asked to conduct a number of Big Data Analytics workshops. The three most common questions have been as follows:

1. What is Big Data and what are others doing with it?
2. How do we build a strategic plan for Big Data Analytics in response to a management request?
3. How does Big Data change our analytics organization and architecture?

Most of the material included in this book was collated in response to answering these questions.

This book provides three perspectives on Big Data Analytics.

First, why is Big Data Analytics becoming so important, and what can we do with it? The book projects major trends behind the rise of Big Data and shows typical use cases tackled by Big Data Analytics, where leading organizations are already seeing major benefits.

Second, the book lists major components of Big Data Analytics and introduces an integrated architecture—Advanced Analytics Platform (AAP)— that combines Big Data Analytics with the rest of the analytics infrastructures and integrates with business processes. It shows how these components work together in the AAP to provide an integrated engine that can combine Big Data with traditional Data Warehouse and Business Intelligence to provide an overall solution.

Third, the book provides a glimpse at implementation concerns and how they must be tackled. How do we establish a roadmap and implement key pilot programs to gather momentum and persist to create a game-changing vision? How do we provide governance across this data when the originating data may have varying quality or privacy constraints?

The big elephant in the room is data privacy. I confess I have not taken a position on data privacy, nor have I predicted how the world will deal with it. It is an evolving topic, with many complications, geographical differences, and unknown consequences. However, I have outlined a number of critical areas to probe further, as well as a number of required components, irrespective of the position taken.

I have relied heavily on my personal work for illustrations of the concepts discussed in this book. As a result, most of the examples are tilted towards CSPs, advertising, and retail industries. This is not to say that these industries are leading the pack or that other industries do not have good Big Data opportunities. To the contrary, we are finding a large number of examples across many industries.

Chapter 2
Drivers for Big Data?

We are increasing the pace for Big Data creation. This chapter examines the forces behind this tsunami of Big Data. There are three contributing factors: consumers, automation, and monetization. More than each of these contributing factors, their interaction is speeding the creation of Big Data. With increasing automation, it is easier to offer Big Data creation and consumption opportunities to the consumers and the monetization process is increasingly providing an efficient marketplace for Big Data.

2.1 Sophisticated Consumers

The increase in information level and the associated tools has created a new breed of sophisticated consumers. These consumers are far more analytic, far savvier at using statistics, and far more connected, using social media to rapidly collect and collate opinion from others. We live in a world full of marketing messages. While most of the marketing is still broadcast using newspaper, magazine, network TV, radio, and display advertising, even in the conventional media, narrow casting is gradually becoming more prominent. This is seen in local advertisement insertions in magazines, insertion of narrow cast commercials using set-top boxes, and use of commuter information to change street display ads. The Internet world can become highly personalized. Search engines, social network sites, and electronic yellow pages insert advertisements specific to an individual or to a micro-segment. Internet cookies are increasingly used to track user behavior and to tailor content based on this behavior.

Email and text messages rapidly led toward increased interpersonal interactions. Communication started not only with marketers but also with third parties and friends. Communication expanded to bulletin boards, group chats, and social media, allowing us to converse about our purchase intentions, fears, expectations, and disappointments with small and large social groups. Unlike email and text, the conversations are on the Web for others to read, either now or later.

So far, we have been dealing only with single forms of communication. The next sets of sources combine information from more than one media. For example, Facebook conversations involve a number of media, including text, sound clips, photos, and video. Second world and alternate reality are becoming interesting avenues for trying out product ideas in a simulated world where product usage can be experimented with.

We often need experts to help us sort out product features and how they relate to our product usage. A large variety of experts are available today to help us with usage, quality, pricing, and value-related information about products. A number of marketers are encouraging advisor or ambassador programs using social media sites. These selected customers get a preview of new products and actively participate in evaluating and promoting new products. At the end of the day, people we know and trust sway our decisions. This is the biggest contribution of social networks. They have brought consumers together such that sharing customer experiences is now far more frequent than ever before.

How would a consumer deal with a poor service quality experience? Figure 2.1 shows typical behaviors in mature and emerging markets as studied by an IBM Global Telecom Consumer Survey conducted with a sample size of 10,177.[7] In this survey, 78 percent of the consumers surveyed in the mature markets said they avoid providers with whom friends or family had bad experience. The percentage was even higher (87 percent) in growth markets. In response to a

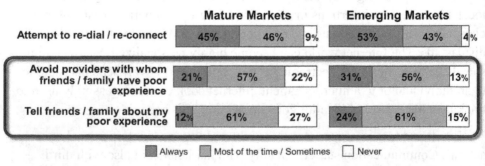

Source: 2011 IBM Global Telecom Consumer Survey, Global N = 10177; Mature Countries N = 7875

Figure 2.1: Behaviors in response to poor service quality experience

related question, survey participants said that they inform friends and family about poor experience (73 percent in mature markets and 85 percent in growth markets). These numbers together show a strong influence of social network on purchase behavior. These are highly significant percentages and are now increasingly augmented by social media sites (e.g., the "Like" button placed on Facebook). The same survey also found that the three most preferred sources for recommendation information are Internet, recommendations from family/friends, and social media.

In any group, there are leaders. These are the people who lead a change from one brand to another. Leaders typically have a set of followers. Once a leader switches a brand, it increases the likelihood for the social group members to churn as well. Who are these leaders? Can we identify them? How can we direct our marketing to these leaders?

In any communication, the leaders are always the center of the hub (see Figure 2.2). They are often connected to a larger number of "followers," some of whom could also be leaders. In the figure, the leaders have a lot more communication arrows either originating or terminating to them compared with others.

How do we identify the leaders? IBM Research conducted a series of experiments with CSPs.[8] Call detail records, which carry information about

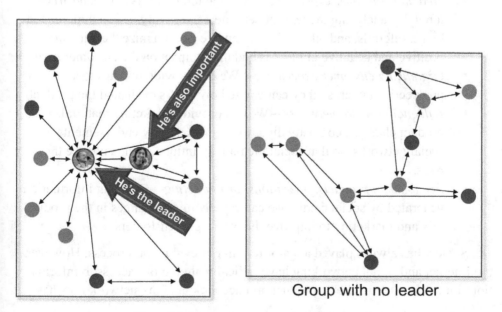

Figure 2.2: Leaders in a communications network

person A calling person B, were analyzed. By synthesizing call information and abstracting communications networks, we discovered webs of communications across individuals. We also used the customer churn information to correlate churn among leaders to subsequent churn among followers. Here are some of the highlights from one of the experiments I helped conduct:

- Leaders were 1.2 times more likely to churn compared with non-leaders.
- There were two types of leaders: disseminating leaders who were connected to their group through outgoing calls, and authority leaders who were connected through a larger proportion of incoming calls.
- When a disseminating leader churned, additional churns were 28.5 times more likely. When an authority leader churned, additional churns were 19.9 times more likely.
- Typically, there was a very limited time between leaders' churn and the followers' churn.

Social groups can be inferred from any type of communication—emails, SMS texts, calls, Facebook friendships, and so on. It is interesting to see strong statistics associated with leaders' influence on the group.

There are many ways to utilize social networks to influence purchase and reuse:

- *Studying consumer experience*—A fair amount of this data is unstructured. By analyzing the text for sentiments, intensity, readership, related blogs, referrals, and other information, we can organize the data into positive and negative influences and their impact on the customer base.
- *Organizing customer experience*—We can provide reviews to a prospective buyer, so they can gauge how others evaluated the product.
- *Influencing social networks*—We can provide marketing material, product changes, company directions, and celebrity endorsements to social networks, so that social media may influence and enhance the buzz.
- *Feedback to products, operations, or marketing*—By using information generated by social media, we can rapidly make changes in the product mix and marketing to improve the offering to customers.

Society has always played a major role in our evaluation process. However, the Internet and social networking have radically altered our access to information. I may choose to "like" a product on Facebook, and my network now has instant access to this action. If I consider a restaurant worth its money, Yelp can help me broadcast that fact worldwide. If I hate the new cell phone service from a CSP, I can blog to complain about it to everyone.

2.2 Automation

Interactive Voice Response (IVR), kiosks, mobile devices, email, chat, corporate Websites, third-party applications, and social networks have generated a fair amount of event information about the customers. In addition, customer interactions via traditional media such as call centers can now be analyzed and organized. The biggest change is in our ability to modify the customer experience using software policies, procedures, and personalization, making self-service increasingly customer friendly.

Sales and marketing have received their biggest boost in instrumentation from Internet-driven automation over the past 10 years. Browsing, shopping, ordering, and customer service on the Web not only has provided tremendous control to users but also has created an enormous flood of information to the marketing, product, and sales organization in understanding buyer behavior. Each sequence of Web clicks can be collected, collated, and analyzed for customer delight, puzzlement, dysphoria, or outright defection. More information can also be obtained about sequence leading up to a decision.

Self-service has crept in through a variety of means: IVRs, kiosks, handheld devices, and many others. Each of these electronic means of communication acts like a gigantic pool of time-and-motion studies. We have data available on how many steps customers took, how many products they compared, and what attributes they focused on, such as price, features, brand comparisons, recommendations, defects, and so on. Suppliers have gained enormous amounts of data from self-service and electronic sensors connected to products. If I use a two-way set-top box to watch television, the supplier has instant access to my channel-surfing behavior. Did I change the channel when an advertisement started? Did I turn the volume up or down when the jingle started to play? If I use the Internet to shop for a product, my click stream can be analyzed and used to study shopping behavior. How many products did I look at? Did I view the product description or the price when looking at the product? This enriched set of data allows us to analyze customer experience in the minutest detail.

What are the sources of data from such self-service interactions?

- *Product*—As products become increasingly electronic, they provide a lot of valuable data to the supplier regarding product use and product quality. In many cases, suppliers can also collect information about the context in which a product was used. Products can also supply information related to frequency of use, interruptions, usage skipping, and other related aspects.
- *Electronic touch points*—A fair amount of data can be collected from the touch points used for product shopping, purchase, use, or payment. IVR tree traversals can be logged, Web click streams can be collected, and so on.
- *Components*—Sometimes, components may provide additional information. This information could include data about component failures, use, or lack thereof. For example, a wireless CSP can collect data from networks, cell towers, third parties, and handheld devices to understand how all the components together provided a good or bad service to the customer.

2.3 Monetization

From a Big Data Analytics perspective, a "data bazaar" is the biggest enabler to create an external marketplace, where we collect, exchange, and sell customer information. We are seeing a new trend in the marketplace, in which customer experience from one industry is anonymized, packaged, and sold to other industries. Fortunately for us, Internet advertising came to our rescue in providing an incentive to customers through free services and across-the-board opt-ins.

Internet advertising is a remarkably complex field. With over $26 billion in 2010 revenue,[9] the industry is feeding a fair amount of startup and initial public offering (IPO) activity. What is interesting is that this advertising money is enhancing customer experience. Take the case of Yelp, which lets consumers share their experiences regarding restaurants, shopping, nightlife, beauty spas, active life, coffee and tea, and others.[10] Yelp obtains its revenues through advertising on its website; however, most of the traffic is from people who access Yelp to read customer experience posted by others. With all this traffic coming to the Internet, the questions that arise are how is this Internet usage experience captured and packaged and how are advertisements traded among advertisers and publishers.

Big Data Analytics is creating a new market, where customer data from one industry can be collected, categorized, anonymized, and repackaged for sale to others:

- *Location*—As we discussed earlier, location is increasingly available to suppliers. Assuming a product is consumed in conjunction with a mobile device, the location of the consumer becomes an important piece of information that may be available to the supplier.
- *Cookies*—Web browsers carry enormous information using web cookies. Some of this may be directly associated with touch points.
- *Usage data*—A number of data providers have started to collect, synthesize, categorize, and package information for reuse. This includes credit-rating agencies that rate consumers, social networks with blogs published or "Like" clicked, and cable companies with audience information. Some of this data may be available only in summary form or anonymized for the protection of customer privacy.

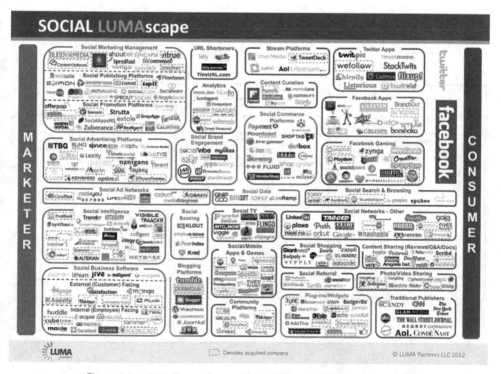

Figure 2.3: LUMA Scape for social media (reprinted with permission)

Terence Kawaja has been studying this market for a number of years and has characterized a number of markets and associated players. "Terence Kawaja has a new way for potential investors to visualize it," says *Wall Street Journal* writer Amir Efrati. "The market involves hundreds of small and large companies that help advertisers reach consumers and help website publishers, mobile-application developers, search engines, and other digital destinations generate revenue through advertising. Kawaja, who runs the investment firm LUMA Partners, spent months putting together six new graphics that show how 1,240 different companies fit into the following categories of online advertising: display, video, search engines, mobile, social, and commerce."[11] I have replicated Kawaja's Social Media LUMA Scape in Figure 2.3. For the rest of the LUMA Scapes, visit Kawaja's website: *www.lumapartners.com*. A number of intermediaries play key roles in developing an advertising inventory, auctioning of the inventory to the ad servers, and facilitating the related payment process, as the advertisements are clicked and related buying decisions are tracked.

Chapter 3
Big Data Analytics Applications

This chapter discusses a number of important use cases for Big Data Analytics. In each case, Big Data Analytics is becoming integrated with business processes and traditional analytics to provide major outcomes. In many cases, these use cases represent game changers essential to the survival and growth of an organization in an increasingly competitive marketplace. Some of these use cases are still in their infancy, while others are becoming increasingly commonplace.

3.1 Social Media Command Center

Last year, Blackberry faced a serious outage when its email servers were down for more than a day. I tried powering my Blackberry off and on because I wasn't sure whether it was my device or the CSP. It never occurred to me that the outage could be at the Blackberry server itself. When I called the CSP, they were not aware of the problem. For a while, I was okay without receiving any emails, but then I started to become curious. So I turned to one obvious source: Twitter. Sure enough, I found information about the Blackberry outage on Twitter.

One of my clients told me that his VP of Customer Service is glued to Twitter looking for customer service problems. Often, someone discovers the problem on Twitter before the internal monitoring organization. We found that a large number of junior staffers employed by marketing, customer service, and public relations search through social media for relevant information. Does this sound like an automation opportunity?

A *Social Media Command Center* combines automated search and display of consumer feedback expressed publicly on the social media. Often, the feedback is summarized in the form of "positive" or "negative" sentiment. Once the feedback is obtained, the marketer can respond to specific comments by entering into a

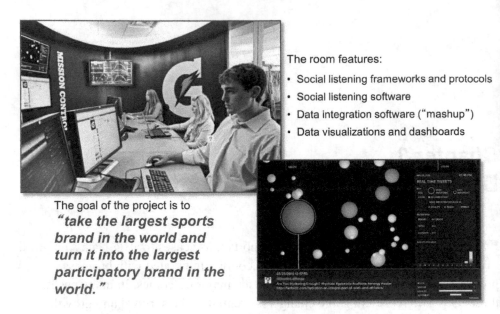

The room features:

• Social listening frameworks and protocols
• Social listening software
• Data integration software ("mashup")
• Data visualizations and dashboards

The goal of the project is to *"take the largest sports brand in the world and turn it into the largest participatory brand in the world."*

Figure 3.1: Gatorade Social Media Command Center

conversation with the affected consumers, whether to respond to questions about an outage or obtain feedback about a new product offering.

The marketing organization for Gatorade, a sports drink product, decided to create a Social Media Command Center to increase consumer dialog with Gatorade.[12] Figure 3.1 shows the monitoring station with the dashboard. Big Data Analytics can be used to monitor social media for feedback on product, price, and promotions as well as to automate the actions taken in response to the feedback. This may require communication with a number of internal organizations, tracking a product or service problem, and dialog with customers as the feedback results in product or service changes. When consumers provide feedback, the dialog can only be created if the responses are provided in low latency. The automated solutions are far better at systematically finding the information, categorizing it based on available attributes, organizing it into a dashboard, and orchestrating a response at conversation speed.

3.2 Product Knowledge Hub

As consumers turn into sophisticated users of technology and the marketplace becomes specialized, the product knowledge seldom belongs to one organization. Take the Apple iPhone as an example. The iPhone is marketed by Apple, but its parts came from a large supply chain pool, the apps running on the iPhone come from a large community of app developers, and the communications service is provided by a CSP. Google's Android is even more diverse, as Google provides the operating system while a cell phone manufacturer makes the device. The smartphones do not work in isolation. They act as WiFi hubs for other devices. So, what happens if I want to know how to tether an iPhone to an Apple iPad? Do I call my CSP, or do I call Apple? Would either of their websites give me a simple step-by-step process I can follow?

Every time I get into these technical questions about products I am trying to use, I end up calling my son, who happens to know the answers to any such question. Recently, he decided to educate me on how he finds the answer, and so I was introduced to a myriad of third-party sites where a variety of solutions can be found. In most cases, we can find them by searching using any popular search engine. However, the solutions do not always favor the CSPs, and they are often dated, failing to take into account the latest offerings. Between the device operating system, the offerings from CSPs, and the apps, one must tread carefully through the versions to make sure the solution we discover is for the same version of software that is on the device. So now, we are facing data that is characterized by both variety and veracity. Can we use Big Data Analytics to solve this problem?

The solution involves three sets of technologies. Fortunately, Vivisimo has packaged these technologies into its Velocity product, making it easier to obtain an integrated solution. The first part of the solution is the capability to tap any sources of data. A CSP may already have pieces of the solution on its intranet, put together by product managers or customer service subject matter experts. Or, the information may reside on a device manufacturer site or a third-party site. All this data must be pulled and stripped of its control information so that the raw text is available to be reused.

The second part of the solution is to create a set of indices so that the raw information can be categorized and found when needed. Because many combinations of products exist, we would like to collect and combine information for the devices searched. The federated indexing system lets us organize the information for easy access.

The third part of the solution involves creating an XML document against a query that can either be rendered by a mashup engine or made available to a third-party application.

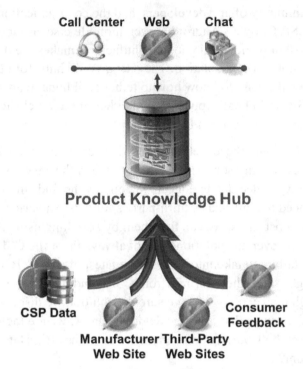

Figure 3.2: Product Knowledge Hub for a CSP

What we have created is a *knowledge hub*, which can now be used directly from a website or made available to the call centers. It significantly reduces call-handling time in the call centers and also increases first call resolution. By placing the information on the web, we are now promoting the CSP's website as the source of knowledge, which increases web traffic and reduces the number of people who resort to contacting the call center. Figure 3.2 depicts the Product Knowledge Hub.

Once we have created a single source of knowledge, this source can be used to upsell other products, connecting usage knowledge to product features and using the knowledge pool to discover new product or business partnership ideas. A lot of stray, fragmented knowledge about the products may be rapidly organized and find a variety of other uses.

3.3 Infrastructure and Operations Studies

A number of industries are exploring the use of Big Data to improve their infrastructure. In many situations, the best way to improve the infrastructure is to understand its use and how bottlenecks or configurations impact performance. In the past, this data required extensive manual data collection costs. Big Data provides a natural source of data with minimal data collection costs. I will lay out examples from public services to illustrate this point.

The city of Boston decided to use Big Data to identify potholes in the streets by sponsoring a competition in the analyst community. A winner came from Sprout & Co., a nonprofit group in Somerville, Massachusetts. The solution included the use of magnitude-of-acceleration spikes along a cell phone's z-axis to spot impacts, plus additional filters to distinguish potholes from other irregularities on the road. The new algorithm made Street Bump, a free download in Apple's App Store, a winner.[13] This analysis can save significant road survey cost. Navigation systems can also use the cell phone data to avoid traffic congestion and offer alternate routes. This type of use of Big Data is one of the best ways to gain acceptance without getting into privacy or security issues.

In another example, city bus and train agencies are making their real-time transit information available to riders. This information significantly improves the user experience and reduces the uncertainty associated with both planned and unexpected delays. Transloc (*www.transloc.com*) provides this information for riders using a variety of technologies, including smartphones, web, and SMS messages. It also provides prediction capabilities on expected arrival time. Once the app is loaded on a smartphone, the rider can use it to accurately estimate travel time and also review the travel route.

IBM's Smarter Cities® initiative is using Big Data in a number of applications directed at city infrastructure and operations. Location data from cell phones can be used to provide raw material for detecting traffic patterns. These patterns can then be used to decide on new transportation projects, to change controls, or to redirect traffic in case of an emergency.

Another important application for Big Data Analytics is public safety. The New York Police Department is using Big Data for crime prevention.[14]

3.4 Product Selection, Design, and Engineering

Product automation provides an enormous opportunity to measure customer experience. We take photos digitally and then post them on Facebook, providing an opportunity for face recognition without requiring laborious cycles in digitization. We listen to songs on Pandora, creating an opportunity to measure what we like or dislike or how often we skip a song after listening to the part of it that we like the most. We read books electronically online or on our favorite handheld devices, giving publishers an opportunity to understand what we read, how many times we read it, and which parts we look at. We watch television using a two-way set-top box that can record each channel click and correlate it to analyze whether the channel was switched right before, during, or after a commercial break. Even mechanical products such as automobiles are increasing electronic interactions. We make all of our ordering transactions electronically, giving third parties opportunities to analyze our spending habits by month, by season, by ZIP+4, and by tens of thousands of micro-segments. Usage data can be synthesized to study the quality of customer experience and can be mined for component defects, successes, or extensions. Marketing analysts can identify micro-segmentations using this data. For example, in a wireless company, we isolated problems in the use of cell phones to defective device antenna by analyzing call quality and comparing it across devices.

Products can be test marketed and changed based on feedback. They can also be customized and personalized for every consumer or micro-segment based on their needs. Analytics plays a major role in customizing, personalizing, and changing products based on customer feedback. Product engineering combines a set of independent components into a product in response to a customer need. Component quality impacts overall product performance. Can we use analytics to isolate poorly performing components and replace them with good ones? In addition, can we simplify the overall product by removing components that are rarely used and offer no real value to the customer? A lot of product engineering analytics using customer experience data can lead to building simplified products that best meet customer requirements.

To conduct this analysis and predictive modeling, we need a good understanding of the components used and how they participate in the customer experience. Once a good amount of data is collected, the model can be used to isolate badly performing components by isolating the observations from customer experience and tracing them to the poorly performing component. Complex products, such as automobiles, telecommunications networks, and engineering goods, benefit from this type of analytics around product engineering.

The first level of analysis is in identifying a product portfolio mix and its success with the customers. For example, if a marketer has a large number of products, these products can be aligned to customer segments and their usage. We may find a number of products that were purchased and hardly used, leading to their discontinuation in six months, while other products were heavily used and sparingly discontinued.

Once we have identified less-used products, the next analysis question is whether we can isolate the cause of customer disinterest. By analyzing usage patterns, we can differentiate between successful products and unsuccessful ones. Were the unsuccessful ones never launched? Did many users get stuck with the initial security screen? Maybe the identification process was too cumbersome. How many users could use the product to perform basic functions offered by the product? What were the highest frequency functions?

The next level of analysis is to understand component failures. How many times did the product fail to perform? Where were the failures most likely? What led to the failure? What did the user do after the failure? Can we isolate the component, replace it, and repair the product online?

These analysis capabilities can now be combined with product changes to create a sophisticated test-marketing framework. We can make changes to the product, try the modified product on a test market, observe the impact, and, after repeated adjustments, offer the altered product to the marketplace.

Let us illustrate how Big Data is shaping improved product engineering and operations at the communications service providers. Major CSPs collect enormous amounts of data about the network, including network transport information coming from the routers and the switches, as well as usage information, popularly known as call detail records (CDRs), which are recorded each time we use telephones to connect with one another. As the CSP networks grew in sophistication, the CDRs were extended to data and video signals using IPDRs. Most CSPs refer to this usage information as xDRs (where x is now a variable that can be substituted for "any" usage information). For larger CSPs, the usage statistics not only are high volume (in billions of transactions a day) but also require low-latency analytics for a number of applications. For example, detecting a fraudulent transaction or abusive network user in the middle of a video download or call may be more valuable than finding out this information the next day. In addition, it is always a strategic driver for CSPs to lay out all the network and usage information on their network topology and geography and use a variety of automated analytics and manual visualization techniques to connect the dots between network trouble or inefficiencies and usage. The analytics provides CSP with a valuable capability to improve the quality of the communication. If every user call is dropping in a particular area that is a popular location for premier customers, it could lead to churn of those customers to competitors.

The information about xDRs, network events, customer trouble tickets, blogs, and tweets in the social media can be correlated for a variety of business purposes. CSPs have used this analytics to detect spots with poor network performance to reorganize towers and boosters. The differences in usage can be analyzed to detect device problems such as faulty antennas on specific models. The variations can also be analyzed to find and fix network policies or routing problems. As CSPs race to implement high-volume, low-latency xDR hubs, they are finding plenty of business incentives to fund these programs and reap benefits in the form of improved product offerings to their customers.

3.5 Location-Based Services

A variety of industries have location information about their customers. Cell phone operators know customer location through the location of the phones. Credit-card companies know the location of transactions, and auto manufacturers the location of cars, while social media is trying its best to get customers to disclose their location to their friends and family. On a recent short trip to India, I decided to use Endomondo, an app on my cell phone to record my jogging activity in Mumbai, India, which was instantly posted on my Facebook page, thereby letting my friends know of my visit to Mumbai.

Let us take a wireless CSP example to study how we collect and summarize location information. A cell phone is served by a collection of cell phone towers, and its specific location can be inferred by triangulating its distance from the nearest cell towers. In addition, most smartphones can provide GPS location information that is more accurate (up to about 1 meter). The location data includes longitude and latitude and, if properly stored, could take about 26 bytes of information. If we are dealing with 50 million subscribers and would like to store 24 hours of location information at the frequency of once a minute, the data stored is about 2 terabytes of information per day. This is the amount of information stored in the location servers at a typical CSP.

Customer locations can be summarized into "hang outs" at different levels of granularity. The location information can be aggregated into geohashes that draw geo boundaries and transform latitude-longitude data into geohash so that it can be counted and statistically analyzed. The presence of a person in a specific location for a certain duration is considered a space-time box and can be used to encode the hang out of an individual in a specific business or residential location for a specific time period.

Many of our smartphone apps collect location data, provided a subscriber "opts-in."[15] If a marketer is interested in increasing the traffic to a grocery store that is located in a specific geohash, they can run an effective marketing campaign by analyzing and understanding which neighborhood people are more likely to hang out or shop in that specific grocery store. Instead of blasting a promotion to all neighborhoods, the communication can now be directed to specific neighborhoods, thereby increasing the efficiency of the marketing campaign. This analysis can possibly be conducted using 6-byte location geohash over a span of one hour and finding all the cell phones that have visited the grocery store regularly. A predictive model can compute the probability of a customer visiting the grocery store based on their past hang out history, and customer residence information can be clustered to identify neighborhoods most likely to visit the shopping center.

Analysis of machine-to-machine transaction data using Big Data technologies is revolutionizing how location-based services can be personalized and offered at low latency. Consider the example of Shopkick, a retail campaign tool that can be downloaded on a smartphone. Shopkick seeks and uses location data to offer campaigns. Once the app is downloaded, Shopkick seeks permission to use current location as recorded by the smartphone. In addition, Shopkick has a database of retailers and their geo-locations. It runs campaigns on behalf of the merchants and collects its revenues from merchants. Shopkick will let me know, for example, that the department store in my neighborhood would like me to visit the store. As a further incentive, Shopkick will deposit shopping points in my account for just visiting the store. As I walk through the store, Shopkick can use my current location in the smartphone to record my presence at the store and award points.

Jeff Jonas provided me tremendous motivation for playing with location data. I used *openpaths.cc*, a site that tracks cell phone location, to track my whereabouts for approximately three months. Watching my movements over these months was like having a video unfold my activities event by event. I could also see how I could improve the accuracy of the location data collected by openpaths with other known information such as street maps. With the help of a business directory, it is easy to find out the number and duration of my trips to Starbucks, Tokyo Joe's, and Sweet Tomato, my three most common eating hang outs.

Why would a customer "opt-in"? Device makers, CSPs, and retailers are beginning to offer a number of location-based services, in exchange for location "opt-in." For example, smartphones offer "find my phone" services, which can locate a phone. If the phone is lost, the last known location can be ascertained via a website. In exchange, the CSP or the device manufacturer may seek location data for product or service improvement. These location-based services could also be revenue generating. A CSP may decide to charge for a configuration service that switches a smartphone to silent mode every time the subscriber enters the movie theater and switches back to normal ring tone once the subscriber leaves the movie theater. Prepaid wireless providers are engaging in location-based campaigns targeted at customers who are about to run out of prepaid minutes. These customers are the most likely to churn to a competitor and could easily continue with their current wireless provider if they were to be directed to a store that sells prepaid wireless cards.

These scenarios raise the obvious data privacy concern, which is a hotly debated topic worldwide. We will spend some time in the technical sections talking about data privacy, governance, and how consumer data can be protected and used only as permitted by the customer. As expected, there are many avenues for abuse of customer data, and data privacy must be engrained in the architecture for an effective protection of customer data.

3.6 Micro-Segmentation and Next Best Action

Automation has provided us with tremendous opportunity to use sensors to collect data in every step of the customer-facing processes, such as click streams in the use of a website. Sensor data gives us an opportunity to establish behavioral patterns using analytics. The early evolution was in use of analytics for segmentation. The original segmentations were demographic in nature and used hard consumer data, such as geography, age, gender, and ethnic characteristics to establish market segmentations. Marketers soon realized that behavioral traits were also important parameters to segment customers.

As our understanding grew, we saw more emphasis on micro-segments—specific niche markets based on analytics-driven parameters. For example, marketers started to differentiate innovators and early adopters from late adopters in their willingness to purchase new electronic gadgets. Customer experience data let us characterize innovators who were eager to share experiences early on and could be more tolerant of product defects.

In the mid-1990s, with automation in customer touch points and use of the Internet for customer self-service, marketing became more interested in personalization and 1:1 marketing. As Martha Rogers and Don Peppers point out in their book *The One to One Future*, "The basis for 1:1 marketing is share of customer, not just market share. Instead of selling as many products as possible over the next sales period to whomever will buy them, the goal of the 1:1 marketer is to sell one customer at a time as many products as possible over the lifetime of that customer's patronage. Mass marketers develop a product and try to find customers for that product. But 1:1 marketers develop a customer and try to find products for that customer."[16]

Early analytics systems were reporting systems that provided raw segmentation data to the marketing team so that they could use the data to decide on marketing activities, such as campaigns. Automation in marketing and operations gave us the opportunity to close the loop—to use analytics to collect effectiveness data to revise and improve campaigns. We are seeing surges in campaign activity. Marketers are interested in micro-campaigns that are designed specifically for a micro-segment or, in some cases, for specific customers. The customer experience information gives us criteria for including a customer in the campaign.

If a marketing analyst were to see my location data, they would immediately conclude that I travel frequently, both domestically as well as internationally. They could establish that when I am not traveling, I am typically working from home and occasionally at an office less than two miles from my house. They could also see a number of my regular activities. At Northeastern University in Boston, network physicists discovered just how predictable people could be by studying the travel routines of 100,000 European mobile-phone users. After analyzing more than 16 million records of call dates, times, and locations, the researchers determined that, when compiled, people's movements appeared to follow a mathematical pattern. The researchers stated that with enough information about past movements, they could forecast someone's future whereabouts with 93.6 percent accuracy.[17]

How do we use location data to derive micro-segments? At the simplest level, if we take the past three months of location data across a set of people, we can differentiate between globe trotters, people doing field jobs, "9 to 5ers" (i.e., people working desk jobs during regular office hours), and people working from home. At the next level, we can start to infer frequent behaviors. By observing how many times I visit a coffee shop, the mall, or a golf course, for example, we can establish my hang outs using frequency rules (e.g., "more than four visits per month, each for a duration of an hour or longer" constitutes a hang out). A marketer may seek a customer to "opt-in" their location information and offer location and context-specific promotions.

Next Best Action (NBA) recommends an activity based on the customer's latest experience with the product. This could include an up-sell or cross-sell based on current product ownership, usage level, and behavioral profile. An NBA could be offered any time the sales organization has the opportunity to connect with the customer via a touch point. NBA is far more effective in sales conversion compared with canned rules that repeatedly offer the same product over and over across a customer interaction channel. (Imagine your airline offering you a discounted trip to your favorite warm-weather golf vacation spot on a cold day.) NBA can also be revised based on feedback from customer reactions.

Let me illustrate how Big Data is changing our business processes. For a number of decades, television producers relied on a control sample of audience viewing habits to gauge the popularity of their television shows. This data was collected using extensive surveys in the early days of television programming and then using special devices placed on a sample of television sets by companies such as Nielsen. With the advancement in the cable set-top box (STB) and digital network supporting the cable and satellite industries, we can now collect channel surfing data from all the STBs capable of providing this information. As a result, the size of data collected has grown considerably, providing us with finer insights not previously available. This information is very valuable because it can be used to correlate channel surfing with a number of micro-segmentation variables.

The grocery stores have been equally busy developing their understanding of customers. Most of them offer frequent shopper cards that can be used by the grocer to track purchase habits as well as used by the shoppers to redeem discounts and other useful campaigns. With identifying information collected from the customer, this shopper card can be correlated with a name and an address. So, if we have the retailer's information from the frequent shopper card and the cable provider's information about television viewing habits, we could correlate the channel surfing data with retail purchases by the household and insert appropriate commercials to run micro campaigns based on household purchases.

Retailers toyed with the idea of providing shopping gadgets to shoppers and eventually realized that creating a smartphone app to run on an existing device would be easier than engineering a new device. The shoppers may activate a mobile app as soon as they enter the retail store. The app starts to collect GPS-level accurate location information about the shopper and lets the shopper check in grocery items on the smartphone. At the checkout counter, the shopper connects the smartphone to the point-of-sale (PoS) device, and the grocery bill is automatically paid by the credit card associated with the app. As the person walks through the grocery store and checks in grocery items using a smartphone, a campaign management system starts downloading mobile coupons based on customer profile, past grocery purchases, and currently active promotions.

While advertising agencies have made the connection via messaging, we now have the ability to connect the dots at micro-segment or one-to-one marketing levels. That is, we can air commercials and see their impact on customer

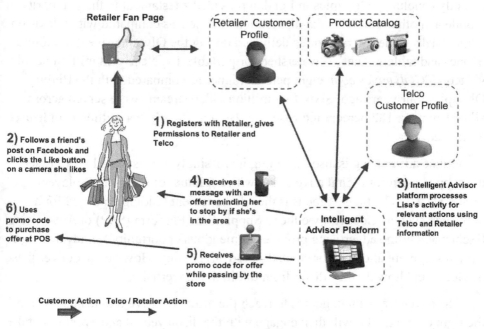

Retailer Fan Page

Retailer Customer Profile

Product Catalog

Telco Customer Profile

1) Registers with Retailer, gives Permissions to Retailer and Telco

2) Follows a friend's post on Facebook and clicks the Like button on a camera she likes

4) Receives a message with an offer reminding her to stop by if she's in the area

6) Uses promo code to purchase offer at POS

5) Receives promo code for offer while passing by the store

Intelligent Advisor Platform

3) Intelligent Advisor platform processes Lisa's activity for relevant actions using Telco and Retailer information

Customer Action   Telco / Retailer Action

Figure 3.3: Intelligent Advisor

purchase, or air commercials based on what a specific consumer is buying. It requires our ability to connect retail and cable advertising data as well as an ecosystem where the two analytics systems (retail and cable) can collaborate.

A triple-play CSP (providing cable, broadband, and wireless services) could use its customer database to correlate customer activities across these three screens. Many consumers are viewing media using Internet over their desktops or tablets. We can now start to correlate media viewing, location-based micro-segments, and customer purchase intentions as known through social media to make retail offers. Figure 3.3 shows a scenario where consumer profiles from CSP and retail segments are used for creating context- and micro-segment-based offers to consumers. The consumer registers on the retailer's website, giving permission to the retailer to use profile data. The retailer uses consumer context and location to tailor a specific promotion.

3.7 Online Advertising

Television and radio have used advertising as their funding model for decades. As online content distribution becomes popular, advertising has followed the content distribution with increasing volumes and acceptance in the marketplace. The recently concluded Olympics in London provided a testament to the popularity of mobile and other online media distribution channels as compared with television. Almost half of the Internet video delivered during the Olympics went to mobile phones and tablets. That's a watershed for portable TV. Nearly 28 million people visited *NBCOlympics.com*, eight percent higher as compared with the Beijing Olympics four years ago. Sixty four million video streams were served across all platforms, a 182 percent increase over Beijing. Nearly 6.4 million people used mobile devices.[18]

Online advertising is also becoming increasingly sophisticated. I discussed the supply chain for digital advertising with a number of specialized players in Section 2.3. The biggest focus is the advertisement bidding managed for a publisher, such as Google, by either a Supply Side Platform (SSP) or Advertising Exchange. Online advertising provides tremendous opportunity for advertising to a micro-segment and also for context-based advertising. How do we deliver these products, and how do they differ from traditional advertising?

The advertiser's main goal is to reach the most receptive online audience in the right context, who will then engage with the displayed ad and eventually take the desired action identified by the type of campaign.[19] Big Data provides us with an opportunity to collect myriads of behavioral information. This information can be collated and analyzed to build two sets of insights about the customers, both of which are very relevant to online advertising. First, the micro-segmentation information and associated purchase history described in Section 3.6 allows us to establish buyer patterns for each micro-segment. Second, we can use the context of an online interaction to drive context-specific advertising. For example, for someone searching and shopping for a product, a number of related products can be offered in the advertisements placed on the web page.

Over the past year, I found an opportunity to study these capabilities with the help of Turn Advertising. Turn's Demand Side Platform (DSP) delivers over 500,000 advertisements per second using ad bidding platforms at most major platforms, including Google, Yahoo, and Facebook. A DSP manages online advertising campaigns for a number of advertisers through real-time auctions or bidding. Unlike a direct buy market (e.g., print or television), where the price is decided in advance based on reach and opportunities to see, the real-time Ad Exchange accept bids for each impression opportunity, and the impression is sold to the highest bidder in a public auction. DSPs are the platforms where all the information about users, pages, ads, and campaign constraints come together to make the best decision for advertisers.

Let us consider an example to understand the flow of information and collaboration between publisher, Ad Exchange, DSP, and advertiser to deliver online advertisements. If a user initiates a web search for food in a particular zip code on a search engine, the search engine will take the request, parse it, and start to deliver the search result. While the search results are being delivered, the search engine decides to place a couple of advertisements on the screen. The search engine seeks bids for those spots, which are accumulated via Ad Exchange and offered to a number of DSPs competing for the opportunities to place advertisements for their advertisers. In seeking the bid, the publisher may supply some contextual information that can be matched with any additional information known to the DSP about the user. The DSP decides whether to participate in this specific bid and makes an offer to place an ad. The highest bidder is chosen, and their advertisement is delivered to the user in response to the search. Typically, this entire process may take 80 milliseconds.

A Data Management Platform (DMP) may collect valuable statistics about the advertisement and the advertising process. The key performance indicators (KPIs) include the number of times a user clicked the advertisement, which provides a measure of success. If a user has received a single advertisement many times, it may cause saturation and reduce the probability that the user will click the advertisement.

As online advertising is integrated with online purchasing, the value of placing an advertisement in the right context may go up. If the placement of the ad results in the immediate purchase of the product, the advertiser is very likely to offer a higher price to the publisher. DSP and DMP success depends directly on their ability to track and match consumers based on their perceived information need and their ability to find advertising opportunities related closely to an online sale of associated goods or services.

3.8 Improved Risk Management

A credit-card company can use cell phone location data to differentiate an authentic user from a fraudulent one. As the credit card is used in a location, the credit-card transaction location can be matched with the cell phone location for the customer to reduce risk of fraudulent transactions.

My work requires me to travel often, almost once a week. Because I travel to a variety of international destinations frequently but use my personal credit card rarely, any purchase with it is very likely to be tagged as unusual activity. This behavior places me under the close scrutiny of the credit-card company's fraud engine because the usage is sporadic and geographically diverse. Invariably, my credit card is occasionally denied at the time of purchase, requiring me to telephone the call center for security verification. I remember talking to a support line three times from India, with each call taking ten minutes or longer. The overall cost of such a call, including telephone charges, the call center agent's time, and my time, adds up significantly.

While I am thankful to the credit-card company for taking my card security seriously, I was curious whether there was an easier way for them to deal with this situation. I asked the credit-card call center agent how I could make the credit-card company's monitoring easier, and the response was to call them before each trip. This solution might reduce the number of times my credit card is denied; however, it would significantly increase the call-center costs. Plus, I would have to make a call every time I traveled, which could be a lot more calls than the number of times my personal credit card is used.

The premise for credit-card fraud is that someone could steal my credit card and use it. A typical fraud rule looks for an unusual purchase initiated in a new international location. Unfortunately, for frequent travelers like me, irregular personal credit-card use can easily mimic these fraudulent transactions. However, I carry a smartphone all the time when I travel. Although my credit-card company may not know of my travel to distant geographies, my smartphone has full awareness of my location. Also, the chances of my losing both my credit card and my phone are significantly lower, and even if someone picked up both, it is highly unlikely they would travel with both credit card and smartphone to make fraudulent purchases. If only I could authorize my credit-card company to check my phone location each time there is a concern about the credit-card usage, and even download an app to my phone that could ask me to authorize the charges using a secure login or password to eliminate the possibility of my phone being stolen at the same time.

Financial institutions are rapidly using smartphones for banking transactions. Today, Chase offers mobile check deposit using the Apple iPhone (see *https://www.chase.com/online/services/check-deposit.htm*). Using my iPhone camera, I can take a picture of both sides of the check and then use the Chase Mobile app on my iPhone to log into my account with a special authorization ID supplied by Chase. Now that my phone and bank are aware of each other, they can use this information for a variety of applications to improve my customer experience.

Chapter 4
Architecture Components

Big Data requires technical capabilities in dealing with velocity, variety, veracity, and volume. A number of emerging applications are scaling to velocity in milliseconds; a variety of unstructured text, sounds, videos, and semi-structured machine-to-machine data; veracity-based weighting; and volumes ranging up to petabytes. This is a tall order and unthinkable in the legacy analytics environment. How do we build these applications, and how do we integrate them with the current environment, which may only be dealing with terabytes of data at "D-1" velocity? A number of architectural components are evolving to deal with these extreme levels of velocity, variety, veracity, and volume. This chapter samples some of the most significant technical components required for Big Data Analytics to work.

I have taken standard components from traditional analytics systems: data ingestion and storage, reporting, master data management (MDM), predictive modeling, and data privacy. For each of these areas, I describe the challenges faced in this brave new world of Big Data. In most cases, we need significant new technical capabilities for extending the current architecture to include Big Data. It is often an easy decision to evolve the current capabilities to include some aspects of Big Data and call it a success. However, as the data tsunami hits the shores, the key question is whether these evolutionary approaches will suffice for ongoing tides of Big Data, or will they get buried in the tide leading to crisis and catastrophic competitive losses. In many industries, business leaders are aggressively turning to Big Data analytics in each of these capability areas to pilot, integrate, or replace the current environment.

4.1 Massively Parallel Processing (MPP) Platforms
Big Data usually shows up with a data tsunami that can easily overwhelm a traditional analytics platform designed to ingest, analyze, and report on typical

customer and product data from structured internal sources. In order to meet the volume challenge, we must understand the size of data streams, the level of processing, and related storage issues. The entire analytics environment must have the capabilities to deal with this data tsunami and should be prepared to scale up as the data streams get bigger.

The use of massively parallel computing for tackling data scalability is showing up everywhere. In each case, the underlying principle is a distribution of workload across many processors as well as storage and transportation of underlying data across a set of parallel storage units and streams. In each case, the manipulation of the parallel platform requires a programming environment and an architecture, which may or may not be transparent to the applications.

Let us start with the platform for large-scale data integration. Any environment facing massive data volumes should seriously consider the advantages of High Performance Shared Service Grid/HA computing as a means to host their data integration infrastructures. Today, the maturity of High Performance Shared Services Grid/Stream/HA computing is such that it is now common, with most companies including it in their strategic planning for architectures and enterprise data centers. The core tenets of Grid/Stream/HA computing are the same as traditional clusters and massively parallel processing (MPP) solutions in terms of the desire to maximize the use of available hardware to complete a processing task. However, what is new about the IBM Information Server Grid/HA and InfoSphere Streams environments is their ease of setup and use, the unlimited linear scalability to thousands of nodes, the fully dynamic load node/pod balancing and execution, the ability to achieve automatic high availability/disaster recovery (HA/DR), and the much lower price points at which you can achieve comparable performance of traditional symmetric multiprocessing (SMP) shared memory server configurations. The overall adoption of grid computing is now becoming commonplace, and it is accelerating, driven by the price-to-performance statistics, flexibility, and economics. The key to the success of the Grid/Stream/HA Shared Service implementations lies in the entire solution working for the business providing straight through processing (STP) with dynamic process allocation, flexibility, and scale-up. A typical parallel data integration platform:

- Designs an integration process without concern for data volumes or time constraints
- Leverages database partitioning schemes for optimal load performance
- Simplifies steps to define partitions within each process if needed
- Uses a single configuration file to add processors and hardware

- Requires no hand coding of programs to enable more processors
- Supports SMP, clustered, grid, and MPP platforms

In InfoSphere Streams, continuous applications are composed of individual operators, which interconnect and operate on one or more data streams. Data streams normally come from outside the system or can be produced internally as part of an application. The operators may be used on the data to have it filtered, classified, transformed, correlated, and/or fused to make decisions using business rules. Depending on the need, the streams can be subdivided and processed by a large number of nodes, thereby reducing the latency and improving the processing volumes.

The Netezza Performance Server (NPS®) system's architecture is a two-tiered system designed to handle very large queries from multiple users. The first tier is a high-performance Linux® symmetric multiprocessing host. The host compiles queries received from Business Intelligence applications and generates query execution plans. It then divides a query into a sequence of subtasks, or snippets, which can be executed in parallel, and it distributes the snippets to the second tier for execution. The host returns the final results to the requesting application, thus providing the programming advantages while appearing to be a traditional database server. The second tier consists of dozens to hundreds to thousands of Snippet Processing Units (SPUs) operating in parallel. Each SPU is an intelligent query processing and storage node and consists of a powerful commodity processor, dedicated memory, disk drive, and field-programmable disk controller with hard-wired logic to manage data flows and process queries at the disk level.

The massively parallel, shared-nothing SPU blades provide the performance advantages of massively parallel processors. Nearly all query processing is done at the SPU level, with each SPU operating on its portion of the database. All operations that easily lend themselves to parallel processing (including record operations, parsing, filtering, projecting, interlocking, and logging) are performed by the SPU nodes, which significantly reduces the amount of data moved within the system. Operations on sets of intermediate results, such as sorts, joins, and aggregates, are executed primarily on the SPUs but can also be done on the host, depending on the processing cost of that operation.

A recent development in the scalability for databases is evident from IBM's pureScale offering. Designed for organizations that run online transaction processing (OLTP) applications on distributed systems, IBM® DB2® pureScale® offers clustering technology that helps deliver high availability and exceptional scalability transparent to applications. Based on technology from IBM DB2 for z/OS®, DB2 pureScale is available as an option on IBM DB2 Enterprise Server Edition and Advanced Enterprise Server Edition, offering continuous availability, application cluster transparency, and extreme capacity.

Hadoop owes its genesis to the search engines, as Google and Yahoo required massive search capabilities across the Internet and addressed the capability of searching in parallel with data stored in a number of storage devices. Hadoop offers the Hadoop Distributed File System (HDFS) for setting up a replicated data storage environment and MapReduce, a programming model that abstracts the problem from disk reads and writes and then transforms it into a computation over a set of keys and values.[20] With the open source availability, Hadoop has rapidly gained popularity, especially in Silicon Valley.

When dealing with high volumes and velocity, we cannot leave any bottlenecks. All the processes, starting with data ingestion, data storage, analytics, and its use, must meet velocity and volume requirements. Some of these systems are designed to be massively parallel and do not require configuration or programming to enable massively parallel activities. In some cases, such as Hadoop, the parallel processing requires programming using special tools, which exploit the parallel nature of the underlying environment (in this case, HDFS). The Hadoop development environment includes Oozie, an open-source workflow/coordination service to manage data processing jobs; HBase for random, realtime read/write access to Big Data; Apache Pig for analyzing large data sets; Apache Lucene for search; and Jaql for query using JavaScript® Object Notation (JSON). Each component leverages Hadoop's MapReduce for parallelism; however, this elevates the skill level required for building applications. To make the environment more user friendly, IBM is introducing a series of tools, such as Big Sheets, that help to visualize the unstructured data.

4.2 Unstructured Data Analytics and Reporting

Traditional analytics has been focused primarily on structured data. Big Data, however, is primarily unstructured, so we now have a couple of combinations available. We can perform quantitative analysis on structured data as before. We can extract structure out of unstructured data and perform quantitative analysis on the extract quantifications. Last, but not least, there is a fair amount of non-quantitative analysis now available for unstructured data. This section explores a couple of techniques rapidly becoming popular with the vast amount of unstructured data and looks at how these techniques are becoming mainstream with their powerful capabilities for organizing, categorizing, and analyzing Big Data.

Figure 4.1: Wordle™ Word Cloud

Search and Count

Google and Yahoo rapidly became household terms because of their ability to search the web for specific topics. A typical search engine offers the ability to search documents using a set of search terms and may find a large number of candidate documents. It prioritizes the results based on preset criteria that can be influenced by how we choose the documents.

If I have a lot of unstructured data, I can count words to find the most commonly used words. Wordle™ (*www.wordle.net*) provides word clouds for the unstructured data provided to it. For example, Figure 4.1 shows a word cloud for the text used in this book. The font size represents the number of times a word was used in the text.

This data can be laid out against other known dimensions. For example, this summer we were working on unstructured data analytics for a CSP in India. We received a large quantity of unstructured text. Our first exercise was to use the Text Analytics capabilities in Cognos® Consumer Insight (CCI) to study key words being used as plotted against time. Figure 4.2 shows the results of this word count plotted against time.

Context-Sensitive and Domain-Specific Searches

Anyone with telecommunications knowledge can easily understand what "3g" and "4g" in Figure 4.2 refer to. Context-sensitive search engines can differentiate between "gold medal" (Olympics) and "gold bullion" (commodity trading). Also, some of the search engines are fine tuned for industry or corporate terms.

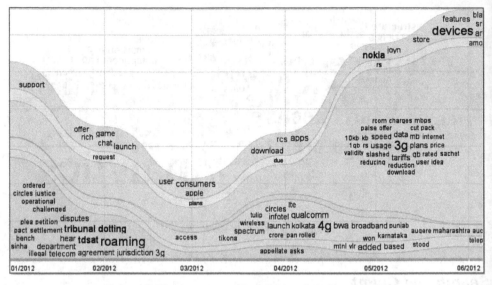

Figure 4.2: Word count graphical display plotted against time

Vivisimo offers the capability to specialize a search engine for a specific purpose, thereby fine tuning it for corporate terms when used inside a corporate intranet.

Categories and Ontology

Often, we like to classify unstructured data into categories. This gives us an understanding of the relative distribution across a known classification scheme. Let me use an example from online purchasing. I use Slice (*www.slice.com*) to keep track of my online purchases. Slice scans my email for any online purchases and extracts relevant information so I can track shipments, order numbers, purchase dates, and so on. Slice also lets me "slice and dice" the orders. That is, it analyzes my purchases against a set of categories to report the number of items and money spent in each category. Figure 4.3 shows Slice's category analysis: Travel & Entertainment, Music, Electronics & Accessories, and so on. Slice must be doing rigorous unstructured analytics to understand what is considered "Movies & TV" and how that is different from "Music."

The classic product categories originated from the Yellow Pages. We remember the classic Yellow Pages books that we received so often and are nowadays getting incorporated into online Yellow Pages and other shopping and ordering tools. However, categories are typically tree structured, where each node is a sub-class of the node above and can be further sub-classified into further specialized nodes. For example, a scooter is a sub-class of two-wheeler, while an electric scooter is a sub-class of scooter. A node can be a sub-class of

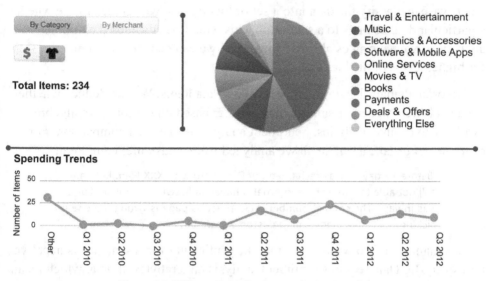

Figure 4.3: "Slice and dice" using product categories

more than one entity. A sub-class shares the attributes of its super-class. Therefore, both scooters and electric scooters should have two wheels. While the classic product catalogs were static and were managed by administrators without organized feedback, the unstructured analytics provides the ability to make a dynamic hierarchy, which can be adjusted based on usage and search criteria.

A more general representation of conceptual entities is found in ontology, which is an abstract view of the world for some purpose.[21] Ontology defines the terms used to describe and represent an area of knowledge. Ontologies are used by people, databases, and applications that need to share domain information (a domain is a specific subject area or area of knowledge, like medicine, tool manufacturing, real estate, automobile repair, financial management, and so on) and may include classifications, relationships, and properties.[22] With formal ontology, we can create a "Semantic Web," which can provide structural extracts to machines, thereby providing them with ability to extract, analyze, and manipulate the data.

Qualitative Comparisons

Once we start to categorize and count unstructured text, we can begin to extract information that can be used for qualitative analytics. Qualitative analytics can work with the available data and perform operations based on the characteristics of the data.

If we can classify the data into a set of hierarchies, we can determine whether a particular data belongs to a set or not. This would be considered a nominal analysis. If we have an established hierarchy, we can deduce the set membership for higher levels of the hierarchy.

In ordinal analysis, we can compare two data items. We can deduce whether a data is better, higher, or smaller than another based on comparative algebra available to ordinal analytics. Sentiment analysis is one such comparison. For example, let us take a statement we analyzed from a customer complaint.

> "Before 12 days, I was recharged my Data Card with XXX Plan. But i am still not able to connect via internet. I have made twise complain. But all was in vain. The contact number on Contact Us page is wrong, no one is picking up. I have made call to customer care but every guy telling me..."

As humans, it is obvious to us that the sentiment of this sentence is negative. However, Big Data requires sentiment analysis on terabytes of data, which means we need to assign a positive or negative sentiment using a computer program. Use of words or phrases such as "I am not able," "complain," "in vain," and "no one is picking up" are examples of negative sentiments. A sentiment lexicon can be used as a library to compare words against known "positive" or "negative" sentiment. A count of the number of negative sentiments is qualitative analytics that can be performed on sentiment data, as we can differentiate between positive and negative sentiment and conclude that positive sentiment is better than negative sentiment. We can also create qualifiers such as "strong" sentiment and "weak" sentiment and compare the two sets of comments.

In typical interval scaled data, we can assign relative values to data but may not have a point of origin. As a result, we can compute differences and deduce that the difference between two data items is higher than another set of data items. For example, a strong positive sentiment may be better than weak positive sentiment. However, these two data items are more similar than the pair of a strong positive and a strong negative sentiment.

Focus on Specific Time Slice or Using Other Dimensions

Data Warehouses are at the receiving end of a large number of transactions. The source data is typically created by a series of (mainframe) applications, which are connected together in a food chain where the output of one program became the input of the next. I studied a data accumulation process where the financial organization was the recipient of these cascading transactions, and the organization needed to balance the books in a short time. If the transactions failed in source systems, the financial reports were likely to be delayed. They were tasked with reducing the number of situations that would lead to delays in data collection. The most common denominators were the system logs from all of these systems.

If we know the past failures in this cascading set of transactions, can we use Big Data Analytics to isolate the failure conditions? IBM's Big Insight includes a query tool that allows us to study a slice of data on a chosen dimension such as time. I can set the time for analysis to be the 24 hours preceding a failure and look for system log error conditions, thereby helping to isolate the combination of error conditions that happened together. If we have located a pattern of error conditions leading to a failure, we can use the query tool to check for all the time slices within system failure and look for any systematic failure patterns.

There are many other use cases where this analysis can be applied. For example, a new pricing model may lead to strong negative sentiment. A new feature release may cause disruption in consumer use. A new competitive offering may reduce interest among shoppers. As long as we have time slices with unstructured data representing independent variables and consumer sentiment as a dependent variable, the data can be analyzed to discover causal chains. This is the most powerful aspect of unstructured data analytics.

4.3 Big Data and Single View of Customer/Product

In any enterprise, there are likely to be many views of customers and products. Most of the fragmentation comes from divergent views of customers and products. Customer and product MDM solutions are popular ways of bridging and bringing together a single unified view. However, over the past decade or two, this integration has been focused primarily on intra-organization sources of traditional "structured" data.

Automation and data collection technologies have opened up new sources of data from the product itself, processes supporting the customers, and third parties. For example, the web interface offers a significant amount of information that can be used for additional customer insight. Tealeaf®, a recent IBM acquisition, specializes in improving multi-channel customer experience by analyzing customer behavior across channels and making that information centrally available. This information about customer behavior at the web interface can now be used for a variety of purposes. It can be used by the contact centers to improve their response to the customers, by product management to improve products, and by IT to improve customer touch points.[23] If the customer has logged into the website, the customer identity is known and can be used to connect customer behavior to the rest of the customer MDM. Product usage can also be tracked and collected, summarized, and categorized. For example, call detail records collect calling information for cell phones. These records carry fairly detailed information, such as cell towers used to make the call, which can be used to pinpoint customer location at the time of the call. The CDR data can be used to understand customer behavior. The device ID is often already connected with the rest of the customer MDM, and the behavior collected from the CDR data can augment the rest of the customer MDM.

With the wide availability of external data, we have opened up the customer and product masters to also include external sources, including Twitter, Facebook, Yelp, You Tube, other blogs, and in general any information publicly available. The information published externally could include intent to buy, product preferences, complaints, endorsements, usage and other useful segmentation data. This data can be collected, collated, identified with individual customers or segments, and connected with the rest of the customer view.

How do we merge internal and external views to create what we may call a Big Data view of the customer or product? This integrated view is a far more holistic understanding of the customer or product. By analyzing and integrating this data with the rest of the customer master, we can now do a far more extensive household analysis. This data may reveal that while the cell phone is being paid for by the parent, the actual user resides in a college dormitory in a different city and should not be offered promotions for regional stores in the city where the parents live unless the student is visiting the parents for a fall break. Figure 4.4 shows some sample elements of a Big Data customer master. It includes personal attributes, life events, relationships, timely insights, and product interests. These elements provide an enormous opportunity to marketers to target products and improve customer service.

Product data is equally interesting. In section 3.2, I described Product Knowledge Hub as the driving application, and in section 4.2 I discussed product ontology, which can be used to organize product data. If we were to gather information from outside sources regarding a set of products, a product MDM allows us to organize this data for a variety of users, including call centers and the web.

The central technical capability in any MDM product is its ability to match identities across diverse data sources. How do we integrate Big Data with the matching capabilities of the MDM solution? Most MDM solutions offer powerful matching capabilities for structured data. I can use MDM software to match customers based on fuzzy logic and to create new IDs that combine customer data from a variety of sources. These solutions are also providing significant

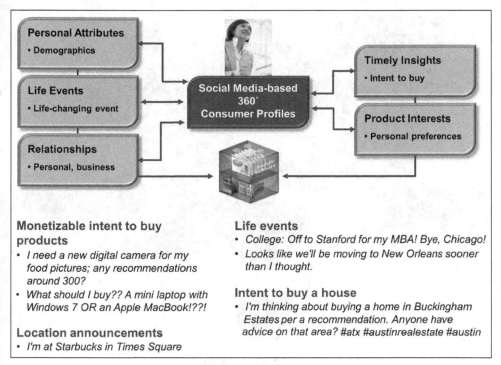

Figure 4.4: Big Data view of the customer

capabilities for using customer and product hierarchies to normalize data across systems. However, in most cases, the format for the data is known and the content is primarily structured. What does source data for Big Data's single view of a customer look like?

Blogs and tweets posted by consumers on social media sites provide a wealth of information for sentiment analysis; however, this data is not structured. Consumers do not always use proper company or product names. The data contains a fair amount of slang words, and there is a mix of languages in a multi-ethnic, multi-language environment. They may use a variety of words to convey positive or negative sentiments. The link to the author is not very well articulated. We start with scant information, such as Twitter handles and unstructured references, and filter and link this data to decipher demographics, location, and other important characteristics required in making this data meaningful to a marketer.

How do we now link the Twitter handle to the customer ID? Obviously, the customer would be the best person to link them together, and customers can sometimes be incentivized to do so with product promotions or information

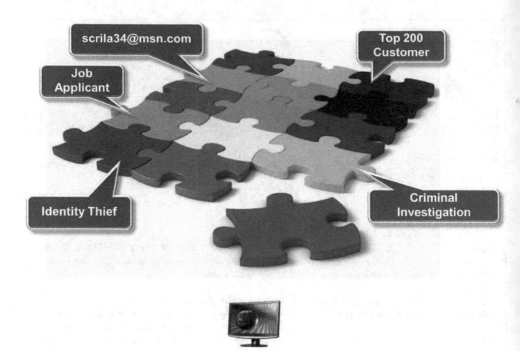

Figure 4.5: Identity resolution

exchange. When such direct means are not available, entity resolution technologies are providing ways to discover and resolve identities (see Figure 4.5).

Identity resolution is the next step in the evolution of matching technologies for MDM. Initially developed by Jeff Jonas for the casino industry, this is a powerful technology that takes into account both normal as well as deceptive data from customers. The technology is based on a set of rules that place the probability of a match on a set of seemingly unrelated facts. As hard facts match, the probabilities are altered to reflect newly discovered information. Customer-initiated actions, such as accepting a promotion, can be hard evidence added to customer handles or user IDs, connecting them to device IDs, product IDs, or customer account information.

Whenever I have made this idea part of a presentation, I have seen several raised eyebrows and questions about customer privacy. Customer privacy is always an area of major concern. For years, corporations collected all types of privacy information and matched it from a variety of sources to obtain a single view of customer. However, most of that information collection was transparent to the customer and happened with full disclosure. Now, however, Big Data has the potential to correlate data across industries and across sources far more extensively than in the past. As a result, privacy is a major issue that I address in the next section.

4.4 Data Privacy Protection

I have banking/investment accounts with five major financial institutions. A major bank recently approached me to consolidate all my banking accounts with them. As we were going through the details, I was being asked to share a fair amount of private information. I wondered how much the bank already knew about me, since I have dealt with them for over a decade and have given them access to credit reports and mortgage applications. Also, a data scientist at the bank could correlate information authorized by me, information publicly available, and self-provided personal information. How is this full and complete view of my customer profile stored and accessed at the bank?

We have heard about data security breaches. Recently, the *Wall Street Journal* published an article about a Yahoo! security breach that exposed 453,000 unencrypted user names and passwords.[24] Is all this data that the bank is collecting about me safe? Often, we assume a large global brand is safe; however, the recent data breaches include a long list of famous brand names.

While an outright data breach is catastrophic and feared by most corporations, predictive models may uncover private facts not yet shared openly and could also lead to privacy loss. Let me illustrate with a famous news story from consumer marketing. Charles Duhigg, a staff writer for the *New York Times*, dug up the process for predicting consumer attributes used by the retailer Target. In his article, he describes how statisticians at Target created a sophisticated customer segmentation model that analyzed customer purchase behavior to predict customer life-cycle stages and related micro-segments. One of the predictive models was a "pregnancy-prediction" model that could predict with reasonable accuracy whether the customer making the purchase was expecting a baby. Unfortunately, the resulting Target campaign reached a house with a girl in high school, and her father decided to make a visit to the Target store. "My daughter got this in the mail!" he said. "She's still in high school, and you're sending her coupons for baby clothes and cribs? Are you trying to encourage her to get pregnant?" The manager at Target promptly initiated an investigation to understand how the campaign was mailed to this girl. However, in a later communication, the girl's father apologized, stating, "I had a talk with my daughter. It turns out there's been some activities in my house I haven't been completely aware of. She's due in August. I owe you an apology."[25]

The data privacy for Big Data is a serious business and is causing regulators around the globe to set up a variety of policies and procedures. Recently, the U.S. Federal Trade Commission settled a case with Facebook that now requires Facebook to conduct regular audits. Facebook, Inc., agreed to submit to the government audits of its privacy practices every other year for the next two decades. The company also agreed to obtain explicit approval from users before changing the type of content it makes public.[26] Similar processes have been put in place at MySpace and Google. In many cases, consumers trade their privacy for favors. For example, my cable/satellite provider sought to have my channel click information shared with a search engine provider. They offered me a discount of $10 if I would "opt-in" and let them monetize my channel surfing behavior.

This leads us to several interesting possibilities. Let us say that a data scientist uses the channel surfing information to characterize a household as interested in sports cars (for example, through the number of hours logged watching Nascar). The search engine then places a number of sports car advertisements on the web browser used by the desktop in that household and places a web cookie on the desktop to remind them of this segmentation. Next, a couple of car dealers pick up this "semi-public" web cookie from the web browser and manage to link this information to a home phone number. It would be catastrophic if these dealers were to start calling the home phone to offer car promotions. When I originally opted in, what did I agree to opt-in to, and is my cable/satellite provider protecting me from the misuse of that data? As we move from free search engines to free emails to discounted phones to discounted installation services, all based on monetization of data and advertising revenue, there is money for everyone, if the data is properly protected against unauthorized use.

The first part of the solution is a data obfuscation process. Most of the time, marketers are interested in customer characteristics that can be provided without Privately Identifiable Information (PII)—that is, uniquely identifiable information about the individual that can be used to identify, locate, and contact an individual. We can possibly destroy all PII information, which may still provide useful information to a marketer about a group of individuals. Now, under "opt-in," the PII can be released to a selected few, as long as it is protected from the rest. In the preceding example, by collecting $10, I may give permission to a web search engine to increase sports car advertisements to everyone in my Zip+4 while at the same time expecting protection from dealer calls, which require a household-level granularity. We can provide this level of obfuscation by destroying PII for house number and street name while leaving Zip+4 information in the monetized data.

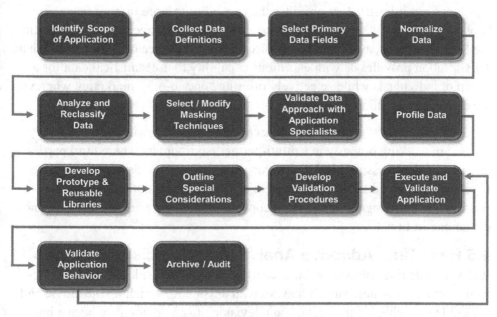

Figure 4.6: Data masking process

As we worked on the data obfuscation process, we found that this process is a lot more complex than expected. While PII data is destroyed, we cannot leave related information that, if joined with obfuscated data, might lead to the individual. For example, if we destroyed the address and phone number but left location information, someone could use the location information to establish the residential address. Also, there are grades of PII information. Zip+4 or county designation may be an appropriate locater unless we are dealing with home addresses of billionaires. Also, small samples are a problem. The non-PII information could uniquely identify an individual if only one individual meets the profile. IBM has been investing in data masking products and processes, which allow us to systematically identify PII information in a data set, tag it, select masking algorithms, test the masking process, and establish the effectiveness of the masking solution (see Figure 4.6 and details on the USPTO site[27]).

Data masking algorithms are equally interesting. The algorithm should remove or randomize PII but not destroy statistical patterns required by a data scientist. For example, if we take a set of real addresses and replace them with XXX, anyone looking for statistical patterns along geographic boundaries would not be able to use the obfuscated data. We have developed a number of algorithms that preserve the uniqueness of the IDs or the statistical patterns while obfuscating the PII data in groups.[28]

A privacy infrastructure provides the capability to store information about "opt-in" and to use it for granting access. Anyone with proper access can obtain the PII information, as granted by the user, while others see only obfuscated data. This solution provides us with enormous capability to use statistical data for a group of individuals while selectively offering "one-to-one" marketing wherever the consumer is willing to accept the offers.

An audit can test whether the obfuscation process, algorithms, and privacy access are working properly in a multi-partner environment where third parties may also have access to this data. If properly managed, the data privacy framework provides gated access to marketers based on permission granted by the consumer and can significantly boost consumer confidence and ability to finance data monetization.

4.5 Real-Time Adaptive Analytics and Decision Engines

As I was watching a movie online recently, the website displayed an advertisement every 10 minutes. Since I had not paid anyone for watching the movie and am used to watching commercials on television, it should not have been a big deal to see a commercial every 10 minutes or so. The website, however, decided to show me the same commercial over and over. After about the fifth time, I felt sorry for the poor advertiser (one of the two U.S. presidential candidates) because the effectiveness of the ad had long since dissipated and, instead, an annoyance factor had crept in. I was facing a real-time decision engine that was rigid and was placing an advertisement without any count or analysis of saturation factor. (As an aside, I live in a "swing state" for the fall 2012 U.S. presidential elections, so it is possible the advertising agency for the candidate had decided to saturate the Internet advertisements to my location.)

How do we build real-time decision engines that are based not on static rules but on real-time analytics and are adaptive, introducing changes as they are executed? In real-time ad placement, a number of factors could have been used as input using information already available to the website that was offering me the movie. For example, the site was well aware of the movie genre I had accessed during several visits to the site. An analysis of this genre could have placed me in several viewing segments. In fact, the same website offers me movie recommendations, which are based on prior viewing habits. This recommendation engine could be offered to the marketers in placing advertisements that match my viewing habits.

Advertisements saturate over a given number of times, after which any additional viewing is ineffective. The website could count the number of times an ad was displayed and decrement the likeness score for the specific ad each time it was shown, thereby favoring a different advertisement to be shown after a certain number of views. A number of sophisticated marketing experiments can be run to effectively control the saturation effect.

After watching the movie for a while and repeatedly viewing the same advertisement, I decided to take a break to search for a food processor as a gift to my son. When I returned to watching the movie, I again faced the same advertisement. I had secretly hoped that my food processor search would conveniently trigger an advertisement for a good food processor to help me in my purchase. By sensing and analyzing my previous web searches, marketers could have offered me appropriate information or deals, thereby increasing the advertisement relevance for me.

It seems there are two sets of input variables that constantly impact the success of advertising. The first includes search context, saturation, and response to advertisement and is fast-moving and must be tracked in real-time. The second set includes viewing habits, shopping behaviors, and other micro-segmentation-related variables and is either static or changes gradually, accumulating over a long time period.

How would real-time adaptive analytics and decision engines acquire the background and accommodate changes to the models while at the same time rapidly executing the engine and providing a context-dependent response? There are four components of a real-time Adaptive Analytics and Decision Engine (see Figure 4.7).

A sensor identifies an incoming event with a known entity. If we do not identify this identity, we can create a new one. However, if this is a known entity that we have been tracking, we will use the identifiers in the event to connect it to previous history for this entity. The entity can be an individual, a device (e.g., a smartphone), or a known web browser identified via a previously placed cookie

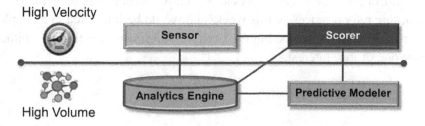

Figure 4.7: Real-time adaptive analytics

or pixel (see note[29] for web tracking technologies). Under opt-in, if we placed a coupon on a smartphone and the person opted-in by accepting the coupon, we may have a fair amount of history about the individual. The analytics engine maintains a detailed customer profile based on past-identified history about the entity. The predictive modeler uses predictive analytics to create a cause-effect model, including impact of frequency (e.g., saturation in advertisement placement), offer acceptance, and micro-segmentation. The scorer component uses the models to score an entity for a prospective offer.

While sensor and scorer components may operate in real-time, the analytics engine and predictive modeler do not need to operate in real-time but work with historical information to change the models. Returning to our example of online advertising, a cookie placed on the desktop identifies me as the movie watcher and can count the number of times an ad has been shown to me. The scorer decrements an advertisement based on past viewership for that advertisement. The analytics engine maintains my profile and identifies me as someone searching for a food processor. The predictive modeler provides a model that increases the score for an advertisement based on past web searches. The scorer picks up my context for web search and places a food processor advertisement in the next advertisement placement opportunity. The sensor and scorer work in milliseconds while the analytics engine and the modeler work in seconds or minutes.

Without a proper architecture, integration of these components could be challenging. If we place all of these components in the same software, the divergent requirements for volume and velocity may choke the software. The real-time components require rapid capabilities to identify an entity and use a number of models to score the opportunity. The task is extremely memory and CPU intensive and should be as lean as possible. On the other hand, the analytics engine and predictive modeler may carry as much information as possible to conduct accurate modeling, including three to six months of past history and the ability to selectively decay or lower the data priority as time passes by or subsequent events confirm purchases against previously known events. I may be interested in purchasing a food processor this week, and would be interested in a couple of well-placed advertisements, but the need will diminish over time as I either purchase one or lose interest.

As we engage with consumers, we have a number of methods to sense their actions, and a number of stages of engagement. A typical online engagement process may track the following stages:

- *Anonymous customer*—We do not know anything about the customer and do not have permission to withhold information.
- *Named customer*—We have identified the customer and correlated to identification information such as device, IP address, name, Twitter handle, or phone number. At this stage, specific personal information cannot be used for individual offers because of lack of opt-in.
- *Engaged customer*—The customer has responded to an information request or advertisement and is beginning to shop based on offers.
- *Opted-in customer*—The customer has given us permission to send offers or track information. At this stage, specific offers can be individualized and sent out.
- *Buyer*—The customer has purchased a merchandise or service.
- *Advocate*—The customer has started to "Like" the product or is posting favorably for a campaign.

A real-time Adaptive Analytics and Decision Engine can help us track a customer through these stages and engage in a conversation to progress a customer from one stage to the next.

Chapter 5
Advanced Analytics Platform

The architecture components described in the previous chapter must be placed in an integrated architecture where they can all coexist and provide overall functionality and performance consistent with our requirements. However, the requirements are at odds with each other. On one hand, we are dealing with unstructured data discovery over very large data sets that may have very high latency. On the other hand, the adaptive analytics activities are bringing the analytics to a conversation level requiring very low latency. How do we establish an overall architecture that respects both of these components equally while establishing a formalized process for data integration? This chapter describes an integrated architecture that responds to these challenges and establishes a role for each component that is consistent with its capabilities. The architecture outlined in this chapter is *Advanced Analytics Platform (AAP)*. We have been experimenting with the integration of architecture components in IBM's Dallas Global Solution Center using a physical implementation of AAP.

I will use an analogy from sports television coverage to demonstrate how this architecture closely follows the working behavior of highly productive teams. I have always been fascinated with how a sports television production is able to cover a live event and keep us engaged as an audience using a combination of real-time and batch processing. The entire session proceeds like clockwork. It is almost like watching a movie, except that the movie is playing live with just a small time buffer to deal with catastrophic events (like wardrobe malfunctions!).

As the game progresses, the commentators use their subject knowledge to observe the game, prioritize areas of focus, and make judgments about good or bad plays. The role of the director is to align a large volume of data, synthesize the events into meaningful insight, and direct the commentators to specific focus areas. This includes replays of moves to focus on something we may have missed, statistics about the pace of the game, or details about the players. At the same time, statisticians and editors are working to discover and organize past information, some of which is structured (e.g., the number of double faults in tennis or how much time the ball was controlled by one side in American football). However, other information being organized is unstructured, such as an instant replay, where the person editing the information has to make decisions about when to start, how much to replay, and where to make annotations on the screen to provide focus for the audience. The commentators have the experience and expertise to observe the replays and statistics, analyze them in real-time, and explain them as they do for the game itself.

The commentators process and react to information in real-time. There cannot be any major gaps in their performance. Most of the data arrives in real-time and is processed and responded to in real time as well. The director has access to all the data that the commentators are processing, as well as the commentators' responses. The director then has to script the next couple of minutes, weighing whether to replay the last great tennis shot or football catch, focus on the cheering audience, or display some statistics. In the course of these decisions, the director scans through many camera views, statistics, and replay collections and synthesizes the next scenes of this live "movie." Behind the scenes, the statisticians and editors are working in a batch mode. They have all the history, including decades' worth of statistics and stock footage of past game coverage. They must discover and prioritize what information to bring to the director's attention.

Let us now apply this analogy to the Big Data Analytics architecture, which consists of three analytics layers. The first is a real-time architecture for conversations; this layer closely follows the working environment of the commentators. The second is the orchestration layer that synthesizes and directs the analysis process. Last, the discovery layer uses a series of structured and unstructured tools to discover patterns and then passes them along to the orchestration layer for synthesis and modeling.

Figure 5.1 maps the Big Data Analytics architecture to the sports television roles.

5.1 Real-Time Architecture for Conversations

Let us start with the low-latency environment first. What are the characteristics of the information alignment and assessment process during a conversation, and how does it differ from the other two layers? How do we ensure that the conversation layer makes rapid inferences and leverages all the hard work by the lower layers?

Conversation layer

Orchestration layer

Discovery layer

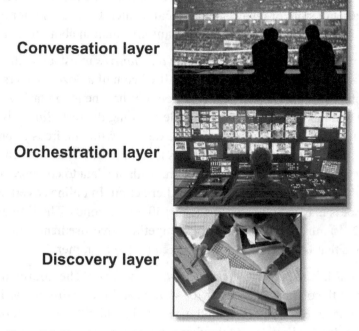

Figure 5.1: Mapping of sports television to Big Data Analytics architecture

Also, how does the orchestration layer guide the conversation layer to make the conversation more relevant and insightful without slowing it down? This section will continue to make use of the sports television analogy and drive it toward characteristics of the architecture and supporting infrastructure of analytics.

The first task at hand is to *identify a situation or an entity*. An analytics system working in conversation mode must use simple selection criteria in the form of counters and filters to rapidly reduce the search space and focus on its identification within a window of time. A television commentator is able to follow the ball, identify the players in the focus area, and differentiate between good and bad performances. Similarly, a real-time campaign system filters all the available data to identify a customer who meets certain campaign-dependent criteria. A customer who has been conducting online searches for smartphones is a good candidate for a smartphone product offer. A number of real-time parameters, such as customer location and recent web searches, would play major roles.

The second task is to *assemble all associated facts*. At this point, the sports television director may offer data previously collected about the players to the commentator, who can combine the data with his or her personal experience to narrate a story. In the Big Data Analytics architecture, the moment a customer walks into a retail store or connects with a call center, the orchestrator uses identifying information to pull all the relevant information about this customer.

The third task is to *score and prioritize alternatives* to establish the focus area. It always fascinates me in U.S. football when half a dozen players wrestle with each other to stop the ball. The commentator has the tough task of watching the ball and the significant players while ignoring the rest. Similarly, in the Big Data Analytics architecture, we may be dealing with hundreds of predictive models. In a relatively very short time (less than one second in most cases), the analysis system must score these models on available data to compare the most important alternative and pass it on for further action. In online advertising, the bidding process may conclude in less than 100 milliseconds. The Demand Side Platform (DSP) must view a number of competing advertisement candidates and select the one that is most likely to be clicked by the customer.

The last task is to *package all the real-time evidence*. The information is turned over to the orchestration layer for storage and future discovery. The conversation layer can now focus on the next task, while the orchestration layer annotates the data and sends it to the discovery layer.

A number of software products are emerging to provide technical capabilities for real-time identification, data synthesis, and scoring commonly referred to as *stream computing*. Stream computing is a new paradigm. In "traditional" processing, one can think of running analytic queries against historical data—for instance, calculating the distance walked last month from a data set of subscribers who transmit GPS location data while walking. With stream computing, one can identify and count, as well as filter and associate, events from a number of unrelated streams to score alternatives against previously specified predictive models. IBM's InfoSphere Streams has been successfully applied to the conversation layer for low-latency, real-time analytics.

5.2 Orchestration and Synthesis Using Analytics Engines

Nowadays, it is impossible to imagine a live television program without orchestration. A highly productive team has replaced what used to be a "sportscaster" in the early days of sports coverage. A typical television production involves a number of cameras offering a variety of angles to the players, in addition to stock footage, commentators, commercial breaks, and more. The director provides the orchestration, assisted by a team of people who organize the resources and facilitate the live event.

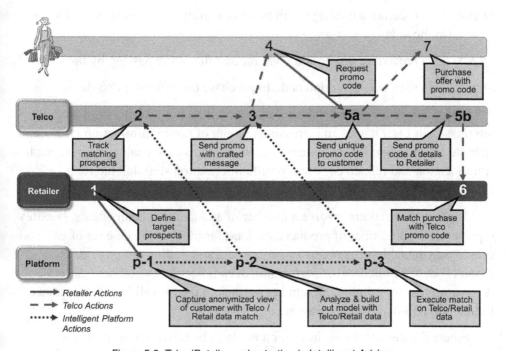

Figure 5.2: Telco/Retailer orchestration in Intelligent Advisor

Similarly, Big Data Analytics is increasingly involving vast amount of components and options. The stakes are becoming increasingly higher. For example, as we discussed in Chapter 3, as new products are launched, there is a need for orchestrated campaigns, where product information is disseminated using a variety of media and customer sentiments are carefully monitored and shaped to make the launches successful.

Let us use the Intelligent Advisor scenario that was described in Section 3.6 and depicted in Figure 3.3. We repeat the steps here so we can analyze the process that the Retailer and Telco use to engage the customer:

Step 1: Lisa registers with the Retailer, gives permission to the Retailer and the Telco to use consumer information to track activities.

Step 2: Lisa follows a friend's post on Facebook and clicks the Like button on a camera she likes.

Step 3: The Intelligent Advisor platform processes Lisa's activity for relevant actions using Retailer and Telco information.

Step 4: Lisa receives a message with an offer reminding her to stop by if she is in the area.

Step 5: Lisa receives a promotion code for an offer while passing by the store.

Step 6: Lisa uses the promotion code to purchase the offer at a PoS device.

Figure 5.2 shows the behind-the-scenes orchestration steps. As the system interacts with Lisa, it uses an increasing amount of opt-in information to make specific offers to her. By the time we get to Step 5, we are dealing with a specific store location and related customer profile information stored in the Retailer's customer database.

These orchestrations involve a number of architectural components, possibly represented by a number of products, each performing a role. One set of components is busy matching customers to known data and finding out more data. Another set of components is performing deep reflection to find new patterns. A management information system keeps track of the overall Key Performance Indicators (KPIs) and data governance.

Figure 5.3 depicts the orchestration model. The observation space and its interactions are in real-time. IBM's InfoSphere Streams provides capabilities suited for real-time pattern matching and interaction for this space. The deep

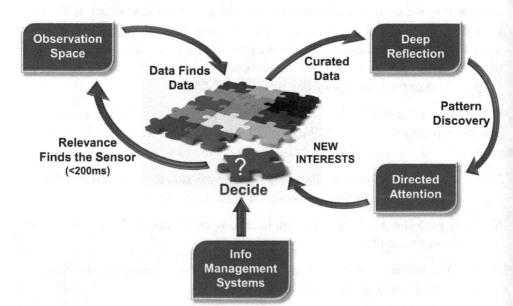

Figure 5.3: Orchestration-driven identity resolution

reflection requires predictive modeling or unstructured data correlation capabilities and can best be performed using SPSS or Big Insights. Directed attention may be provided using a set of conversation tools, such as Unica® or smartphone apps (e.g., Worklight™). Management reporting and dashboard may be provided using Cognos. Depending on the level of sophistication and latency, there are several components for the box in the middle, which decides on the orchestration focus, directs various components, and choreographs their participation for a specific cause, such as getting Lisa to buy something at the store.

Entity Resolution

Using a variety of data sources, the identity of the customer can be resolved by IBM's Entity Analytics®. During the course of the entity resolution, we may use offers and promotion codes to encourage customer participation, both to resolve identity as well as to obtain permission to make offers (as in Steps 4 and 5 above).

Model Management

IBM SPSS provides collaboration and deployment services, which are able to keep track of the performance of a set of models. Depending on the criteria, the models can be applied to different parts of the population and switched, for example, by using the champion/challenger approach.

Command Center

A product manager may set up a monitoring function to monitor progress for a new product launch or promotional campaign. Monitoring may include product sales, competitive activities, and social media feedback. Velocity from Vivisimo, a recent IBM acquisition, is capable of providing a mechanism for federated access to a variety of source data associated with a product or customer. A dashboard provides access to a set of users monitoring the progress. Alternatively, the information can be packaged in an XML message and shipped to other organizations or automated agents.

Analytics Engine

An analytics engine may provide a mechanism for accumulating all the customer profiles, insights, and matches as well as capabilities for analyzing this data using predictive modeling and reporting tools. This analytics engine becomes the central hub for all information flows and hence must be able to deal with high volumes of data. IBM's Netezza product has been successfully used as an analytics engine in Big Data architectures.

5.3 Discovery Using Data at Rest

Statisticians and video editors are the third set of team members in a sports-cast. These people work with a lot of historical data and constantly work on the statistics to compare the current game with past ones. They also capture and edit replays by focusing on the game from a start time to an end time and using multiple camera angles to show the action from different viewpoints.

In the world of Big Data Analytics, statistical models perform structured data analytics, while a number of accelerators have been built for unstructured analysis. For example, query tools in Big Insights can be used to focus on data from one point in time to another and correlate a number of sources, much like the way an editor brings together multiple camera moments in sports television.

Business Intelligence has been focused primarily on structured data. MDM provides the ability to match structured customer or product data to bring a single view of customer or product. Data Warehouses provide the ability to store ingested data and build different data representations for the purpose of reporting or predictive modeling.

The presence of unstructured data brings in a set of data scientists who work with a mix of unstructured and structured data to determine insights. These insights are offered to the orchestration layer and could also be obtained at the command of the orchestration layer focused on specific entities (for example, detailed analytics about the hour before a major network outage, focusing on network entities in the vicinity of the outage).

The discovery layer provides much-needed reflection on the historical data. By nature, discovery is slower than the conversation and orchestration layers. However, the results of discovery can be integrated in the analytics engine with more recent data and used to interpret or augment the conversation. Much as a commentator may use statistics to make a point in the middle of a narration, the discovery layer in the Big Data architecture provides much-needed context and behavioral prediction to a sales conversation in order to provide an offer.

Computers have traditionally been assigned to numeric computing. As a result, structured data analytics using statistical models is a mature topic. We are now seeing the emergence of a couple of unstructured data analytics techniques, as I summarized earlier in the book (in Section 4.2). Let us turn our attention now to how we combine inferences drawn from structured and unstructured analysis and how we use them together for an overall ranking.

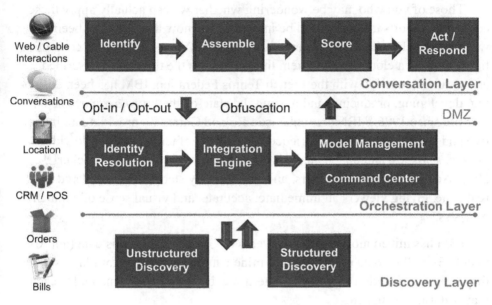

Figure 5.4: Advanced Analytics Platform (AAP)

5.4 Integration Strategies

Once connected together, the integrated Advanced Analytics Platform (AAP) is as shown in Figure 5.4. As we integrate the three layers, we can incorporate a data privacy layer to differentiate between internal and external sources or users. I have placed that layer between the conversation and orchestration layers in this figure to depict conversation on social media sites. However, the privacy layer could go anywhere in this diagram, based on the placement of external sources or users.

The current Business Intelligence environment can be integrated in one of three ways. First, in a typical greenfield Big Data Analytics implementation, we could make the current MDM or warehouse one of the sources and keep the new architecture completely out. Second, the BI environment could provide the structured data discovery component and could be connected to a Big Data Analytics engine. Third, in the most evolutionary approach, the BI environment could provide the orchestration layer and could be augmented with unstructured discovery, identity analytics, and the conversation layer. The first option provides the best architecture to meet Big Data requirements, while the third provides the best leverage of the current investment.

Those of you who may be wondering whether we can actually apply these concepts to sports television will be interested to know that IBM has been working closely with Roland Garros, one of tennis's most celebrated competitions, to build a cloud-based system that automates the three roles described above. In conjunction with the French Tennis Federation, IBM has been designing, developing, producing, and hosting the state-of-the-art *rolandgarros.com* website since 1996.[30] IBM has enhanced Roland Garros by providing an innovative and immersive online experience for millions of tennis fans worldwide. Scores, statistics, and match analysis come to life with IBM SlamTracker™ 2012. Aces, serve speed, winners, and all other key statistics are rendered in real-time, giving viewers an immediate, accurate, and visual sense of a match in progress.

IBM has mined more than seven years of Grand Slam Tennis data (approximately 39 million data points) to determine patterns and styles for players when they win. This insight is applied to determine the "keys" to the match for each player during the match:

- Prior to each match, the system runs an analysis of both competitors' historical head-to-head matchups, as well as statistics against comparable player styles, to determine what the data indicates each player must do to perform well in the match (SPSS technology).
- The system then selects the three most significant keys for each player in the match.
- As the match unfolds, the Keys to the Match dashboard updates in real-time with current game statistics.

Fans will find their voice within SlamTracker, adding comments about featured matches through Facebook and Twitter.

Chapter 6
Implementation of Big Data Analytics

This chapter provides glimpses of implementation plans and related challenges. Big Data Analytics may disrupt a major BI program. Do we use Big Data Analytics to radically transform this organization or evolve it for balanced growth? How do we establish a road map and find initial pilots? How do we evolve data governance to include considerations for Big Data?

6.1 Revolutionary, Evolutionary, or Hybrid

A typical Big Data Analytics implementation delivers three significant advancements in performance. First, it can reduce latency by an order of magnitude, providing accessibility to data in minutes or seconds as opposed to hours or days. Second, it increases the capacity to store data by an order of magnitude, moving from terabytes to petabytes. Third, it offers a much lower cost of acquisition and operation. Because the architecture is typically built on commodity hardware and requires fewer administrators, the cost, too, is reduced by an order of magnitude.

However, these implementations require a commitment to Big Data Analytics and a strong desire to migrate from the current platform. What if we have already invested a large IT budget in conventional BI? How far do we go in the first phase? Do we replace the current Data Warehouse architecture or augment it with Big Data Analytics tools? Both approaches have obvious pros and cons. In this section, I describe the three alternatives and discuss what would tilt us in one direction or another for a specific implementation.

Before I review the alternatives, let us first place the current environment in the context of the architecture described in Chapter 5 and understand how similar or dissimilar the architectures are.

In a typical "traditional" architecture, we have a set of components for ingesting data, a set of components for storing the data, and a set of components for analyzing the data and then feeding the results into a set of actions or reports. Since all the data must be routed via a storage medium using a data warehouse, the storage, organization, and retrieval of data creates a bottleneck. Typically, the traditional approach requires a reorientation of the data from the data source to a system of record and then into a set of models conducive to analytical processing—which typically requires a number of data modelers, database administrators, and ETL analysts to maintain the various data models and associated keys. Changes to the business environment require changes to models, which cascade into changes across each component and require large maintenance organizations.

Many components have already started to break off from this traditional model. Netezza as the Data Analytics engine does not strictly follow this paradigm, and it significantly reduces the model maintenance costs by reducing the need for representation and key-driven performance tuning. Use of SPSS and Cognos as user interfaces to drive modeling and reporting using Netezza's data manipulation capabilities reduces the repopulation of data in analytics tools.

The *revolutionary* approach involves creating a brand-new Big Data Analytics environment. We move all the data to the new environment, and all reporting, modeling, and integration with business processes happens in the new environment. This approach has been adopted by many greenfield analytics-driven organizations. They place their large storage in the Hadoop environment and build an analytics engine on the top of that environment to perform orchestration. The conversation layer uses the orchestration layer and integrates the results with customer-facing processes. The stored data can be analyzed using Big Data tools. This approach has provided stunning performance but has required high tooling costs and skills.

In a typical *evolutionary* approach, Big Data becomes an input to the current BI platform. The data is accumulated and analyzed using structured and unstructured tools, and the results are sent to the data warehouse. Standard modeling and reporting tools now have access to social media sentiments, usage records, and other processed Big Data items. Typically, this approach requires sampling and processing Big Data to shelve the warehouse from the massive volumes. The evolutionary approach has been adopted by mature BI organizations. The architecture has a low-cost entry threshold as well as minimal impact on the BI organization, but it is not able to provide the significant enhancements seen by the greenfield operators. In most cases, the type of analysis and the overall end-to-end velocity is limited by the BI environment.

The *hybrid* approach promoted actively by IBM's Information Agenda team places the AAP architecture on top of existing BI infrastructure. All the Big Data flows through AAP, while conventional sources continue to provide data to the data warehouse. We establish a couple of integration points to bring data from the warehouse into the analytics engine, which would be viewed by the data warehouse as a data mart. A sample of the AAP data would be directed back to the data warehouse, while most of the data would be stored using a Hadoop storage platform for discovery. The hybrid architecture provides the best of both worlds; it enables the current BI environment to function as before while siphoning the data to the AAP architecture for low-latency analytics. Depending on the transition success and the ability to evolve skills, the hybrid approach provides a valuable transition to full conversion.

Both the revolutionary and the hybrid architectures significantly challenge the data governance function. The next section describes the new set of issues and how to handle them.

6.2 Big Data Governance

Three broad categories of questions are emerging in the area of Big Data governance:

- *Single view of the customer*—We now have access to more complete data on how customers use their products for their communications, content, and commerce needs. How do we merge this newly acquired data with everything else we have been collecting to create a more comprehensive understanding of the customer?
- *Big Data veracity*—Customer data comes from a variety of "biased" samples with different levels of data quality. How do we homogenize this data, so that it can be used with confidence?
- *Information lifecycle management*—This is a lot more data than we have ever encountered before. Our current analytics systems are not capable of ingesting, storing, and analyzing these volumes at the required velocities. How do we store, analyze, and use this data in real-time or near real-time?

We will use this chapter to elaborate on these questions and will provide partial answers as they are known today.

Integrating Big Data with MDM

During the 1980s and 1990s, we created a series of departmental applications based on business cases associated with workforce automation. The result was a series of departmental databases containing customer, product, and related data. While the billing and sales views were often overlapping in these applications, it was not easy to map one to the other.

The past 10 years have seen a rapid rise in MDM for customer and product data across the enterprise. Analytics applications were the first consumers of master data to create mappings across multiple hierarchies as well as fragmented customer and product identifiers. MDM then graduated to transactional applications with much of the focus on business solutions, specifically customer relationship management (CRM) and billing systems. We can now use Big Data to build a comprehensive view of customer, network, and external data as demonstrated in the following case study.

Jim and Mary Smith have two children, Corey and Karen. The family has four phones, one for each family member. Corey and Karen are in high school and have basic phones for calls and text. Jim has an iPhone, which he uses primarily for office calls and emails. Mary has an iPhone and a WiFi-only iPad. She uses her iPad for investment research and participates in financial blogs.

When Jim received a brand-new iPhone from his employer as part of an upgrade program, he decided to give his older iPhone to Karen. Karen decided to sell her basic phone to a friend. Since they were in the last six months of their contract, the Smith family decided to keep the friend's phone on their plan until the end of the period. Karen's friend paid her for basic phone and messaging service.

The CSP providing phone service to the Smiths had done extensive household analysis to develop a customer hierarchy of their residence that tagged phones to users and connected all the users to the family account. After the changes mentioned above, the CSP's analytics applications would likely display abnormal calling patterns for the users compared with historical norms. In addition, Jim's old iPhone would show a number of web transactions that tracked to Jim's user ID but exhibited web browsing behaviors that were characteristic of a teenager. Karen's phone is now "hanging-out" in a new geohash.

Network data provides the best view of customer usage and trouble information. If this data is harnessed and offered as a strategic asset to others in the organization, it can provide a far more comprehensive understanding of the customer. In many cases, it may not even be important to connect the phone exchanges to the PII. The location and usage patterns may provide valuable insights about the user. The resulting view of customer hierarchies and house-holds is far more accurate.

This case study would be even more dynamic if Karen were to borrow Jim's phone during a trip for a day or two. In growth markets, providers of prepaid services see massive churn in their customer base as consumers switch suppliers based on costs. The usage information can be used to track down a subscriber even as he or she switches telephone numbers. From a governance perspective, we must establish how the Big Data customer profile would be maintained, used, and integrated with the rest of MDM.

Big data brings new challenges to data quality management. If properly governed and managed, internal data quality can be measured and managed. Unfortunately, we have less control over the management of external data. However, it is even more important that we assess the value of the external data and its data quality. Merging of internal and external data should be done carefully based on an understanding of the quality of the external data and an appreciation for how the merged data will be used. Let us consider the following regarding the use of Twitter data.

A marketer launches a new product nationally and observes data relating to product sales, trouble tickets, network usage, and Twitter. A number of Tweets show consistently negative sentiments from Twitter users for the product. We are concerned that the data is an anomaly because sales of the product are brisk and there has been no significant increase in the number of trouble tickets.

Why is the Twitter data so out of whack? A closer analysis shows that older customers are relatively happy with the product and use surveys and trouble tickets to provide feedback. On the other hand, the product is not doing well with younger customers. The younger customers do not rely on traditional means of feedback and have been using Twitter to discuss the product in a negative way.

Because social media information is mostly self-reported, it is somewhat more prone to biased sampling. As a result, we must adopt a process to deal with Big Data quality during data aggregation. We must report the overall confidence level with the data, especially if it does not represent the entire population.

Big data can mean big storage, assuming all the data needs to be stored. Contrary to traditional data warehousing and analytics, we can perform Big Data Analytics at the time of data collection. As a result, we may need to maintain only a smaller subset, such as samples, filters, and aggregations in tier one storage.

Big data also provides its own tier two storage environment. Large quantities of unstructured data can be placed in Hadoop, which can be MapReduced later for any meaningful insight. A number of query tools are now available for large-scale queries on this data.

At the beginning of this chapter, we raised three questions for which we have provided partial answers as summarized below:

- *Single view of the customer*—We now have access to more complete data on how customers use their products for their communications, content, and commerce needs. As we merge this newly acquired data with everything else, we must closely monitor how the data is being used and how it is being aggregated. All this occurs as we radically change the rules on data privacy, redefine MDM, and encounter new concerns relating to data quality.
- *Big data quality*—Customer data comes from a variety of "biased" samples with different levels of data quality. As we homogenize this data, we must establish confidence levels on raw data, as well as aggregations and inferences, in order to understand and remind users of the "biases" built into the sourced data.
- *Information lifecycle management*—This is a lot more data than we have ever encountered before. Our current analytics systems are not capable of ingesting, storing, and analyzing these volumes at the required velocities. We may decide to store only samples of the data or use Hadoop for the storage and retrieval of large volumes of unstructured data.

We have explored a number of case studies, observations, and solutions in the chapter. This is a new field, and organizations are breaking new ground in terms of Big Data governance. We are sure to find new solutions to data quality, MDM, data privacy, and information lifecycle management as we deal with Big Data governance.

6.3 Journey, Milestones, and Maturity Levels

Big Data Analytics is a journey. What may be a bleeding-edge capability for one company or industry may be the base-level criteria for staying in business for another. This section describes a maturity model that allows us to measure the milestones in this journey so that we can benchmark a company in comparison with its peers. In Chapter 3, we discussed a number of business use cases. The maturity model can be applied to each of those use cases to help us measure the level of solution sophistication and the relative impact on KPIs. We can use the maturity model to represent the target state, current state, gaps, and relative maturity of the industry and competition.

Drivers are either internal or external forces that drive senior management priorities. For a commercial enterprise, factors such as revenue, cost, and customer acquisition and retention are typical drivers for its management to drive the organization's market valuation. For a government entity, the welfare and protection of citizens are typical drivers for analytics. For financial institutions, risk management is a key driver.

Capabilities represent a collection of business processes, people, and technology for a specific purpose. For example, a financial institution may have a risk management function for loan approval. The risk management would require technology components for statistical analysis and modeling, a set of trained people who can assemble risk management information from a variety of sources, and a risk management process that starts with risk data and ends with a score for a customer. Analytics supports a number of key capabilities in response to drivers. In the past five years, these capabilities have become increasingly sophisticated, as well as automated. Some of these capabilities are inter-organizational. For example, we discussed a set of business scenarios where retailers would collaborate with CSPs. As the amount of data has grown, so have the tools for faster data collection and real-time analytics. These tools have enabled a whole set of new capabilities. Let us examine a set of analytics-supported capabilities to support typical drivers.

Measurements are used to quantify the progress of a capability and its impact. With the increasing automation in products and processes, we now have many more ways to measure the effective functioning of a capability. These measurements can be visualized using a business value tree.

As we evaluate an analytics program, measurements help us visualize the capabilities required and their impact, thereby allowing management to prioritize program spending based on the capabilities that have the biggest impact to the organization. Measurements are used to link business capabilities to drivers. Value trees can also be used to identify common capabilities that impact multiple measurements and can be used to track benefits by program phases, identifying capabilities enabled by a particular phase. We can also maintain best practices for each capability to estimate the impact of a capability using past case studies.

Analytics Business Maturity Model

As I stated earlier, Big Data Analytics is a journey and can be implemented using a number of iterative phases, each advancing the capability via well-defined yet small steps to reduce risk. The Information Agenda team has observed a large number of analytics programs worldwide and has developed a set of benchmarks for analytics at different levels of maturity. These benchmarks have been captured using a business maturity model that allows us to specify current and target levels of maturity and what can be achieved in each phase. The model has five levels of maturity:

- *Breakaway*—A company that is generally considered to be the best in the class in its execution of key business strategies, able to exhibit the characteristics of an agile, transformational, and optimized organization. This classification excludes "bleeding-edge" or pioneering aspects; however, these aspects may also be evident in such companies. Key predictive performance indicators are used in modeling for outcomes, and information is utilized enterprise-wide for multidimensional decision making.
- *Differentiating*—A company whose execution of key business strategies through utilization of information is viewed as generally better than most other companies, creating a degree of sustainable competitive advantage. Management has the ability to adapt to business changes to a degree, as well as measure business performance. Business leaders and users have visibility to key information and metrics for effective decision making.
- *Competitive*—A company whose capabilities generally are in line with the majority of similar companies, with a growing ability to make decisions on how to create competitive advantage. This maturity level is also the starting point to establish some consistency in key business metrics across the enterprise.
- *Foundational*—A company whose capabilities to gather key information generally lag behind the majority of its peers, which could potentially result in a competitive disadvantage. Information is not consistently available or utilized to make enterprise-wide business decisions. A degree of manual efforts to gather information is still required.

	Ad hoc	Foundational	Competitive	Differentiating	Breakaway
Capability: Monitor brand sentiment	Marketing has hired a set of interns to monitor social media data	Organizational accounts to collect sentiment data on social media sites (Facebook, Yelp, etc.)	Customer data from social media is collected and analyzed using analytical tools	Organization engages in social media conversation to influence customer sentiment	Customer sentiment is integrated with product and marketing processes
Measurements					
Brand sentiment	Baseline	Collected	Measured	Influenced to positive direction	Influenced to positive direction
Identification of advocates / ambassadors	Baseline	Low	Medium	High	High
Impact on brand / revenue	Baseline	Baseline	Small	Medium	Large

Figure 6.1: Social media maturity model

- *Ad hoc*—A company that is just starting to develop the capability to gather consistent information in key functional areas, generally falling well behind other companies in the corresponding sector. Information beyond basic reporting is not available. Time-consuming, manual efforts are generally required to gather the information needed for day-to-day business decisions.

This model is an important tool in developing an enterprise-wide analytics roadmap. It allows us to specify specific capabilities developed in each phase, compare them with others in the industry, and align metrics to each level, so that the benefits can be identified using the metrics and can be quantified using either benchmarks or company-specific information.

The business maturity model lets us rapidly quantify the benefits of an analytics program. We have been tracking actual benefits using case studies and using these benchmarks in roadmap development. The maturity models and their underlying descriptions are industry-specific, as implementations and benefits differ from one industry to the next.

Figure 6.1 shows an example of the maturity model applied to the capability Monitor Brand Sentiment. At the Foundational level, the marketing organization establishes a Facebook account, which is used by customers to express sentiments; however, the sentiment information is not used in any way. At the Competitive level, the organization establishes a mechanism for collecting, collating, and analyzing sentiment and tracking its value with the marketing events. At this stage, the sentiment is measured but not actively managed.

Lisa Mancuso, SVP of Marketing for Fisher-Price, recently talked about the company's ambassador program in an interview with *Forbes* magazine. "We know that more than two-thirds of mothers consider blogs to be a reliable resource for parenting information, so we have created a robust program to connect with parenting bloggers around the world. We call them our Play Ambassadors."[31] Such programs, when actively integrated with social media accounts, give organizations the capability to start differentiating themselves in their ability to converse with the customers.

At the Breakaway level, sentiments from social media are linked to the product and marketing processes. Sentiments are monitored in response to a product launch, pricing, changes, or a new advertising campaign. The results are directed to product and marketing processes to modify the product and its marketing. Successful marketers would use social media as a channel to experiment with different product options and use the feedback to launch the one with the best customer response.

Chapter 7
Closing Thoughts

I started this book with a definition of Big Data using the four V's: Velocity, Volume, Variety, and Veracity. Big Data growth can be attributed to three market forces: sophisticated consumers, product and process automation, and data monetization. I discussed a number of emerging use cases, including location-based services, micro-segmentation, next best action, Product Knowledge Hub, Social Media Command Center, infrastructure and operation improvement, and risk management. The solution includes a number of architecture components. Massively parallel platforms provide capabilities for data integration, storage, and analytics. Unstructured text analytics complements traditional quantitative modeling. Big data enhances the creation of customer and product MDM. Real-time adaptive analytics provides high-velocity analytics while changing its modeling parameters based on sophisticated predictive modeling of historical data.

I discussed data privacy issues and how some of the data can be masked to limit exposure. These components can be organized in a three-layer architecture, with a conversation layer that uses real-time analytics to provide low-latency decisions and an orchestration layer that synthesizes entities, controls the conversation, and offers visibility to business users via a command center. The supporting discovery is provided by unstructured and structured analysis. Last, I discussed implementation approaches, data governance, roadmap development, and maturity models.

By calling it "Big Data," our attention obviously goes first to the volume dimension. With data sizes in exabytes, the analytics requires special tools capable of scaling to such big volumes. We saw how massively parallel platforms provided performance that naturally scales. The HDFS platform offers inexpensive data storage but requires special skills to manipulate the data. Also, as we collect more data, we increase our chances of improved identity resolution.

The velocity dimension forces us to establish an architecture where conversations can be intelligent and yet fast enough to handle the velocity requirements for the use cases. Location-based campaigns and web searches are two examples of capabilities that require low-latency response. Real-time adaptive analytics provides a robust architecture to deal with low-latency analytics while at the same time adjusting the models to accommodate changes based on historical and predictive modeling. The orchestration layer allows us to converse intelligently based on historical data, sophisticated models, and both unstructured and structured discovery.

The variety dimension focuses on unstructured data. A number of qualitative reasoning techniques can be used in conjunction with quantitative predictive modeling to incorporate findings from the unstructured data in the predictive models. In addition, qualitative reasoning in the context of time-based correlations allows us to find a specific collection of events.

The veracity dimension focuses on data quality, governance, and privacy-related issues. By incorporating a proper governance framework, we can identify faulty data and discount it before creating predictive models. The result is a thorough cleanup of the data before it is used in a critical customer-facing situation.

We looked at a number of use cases. Use of Big Data has enormous potential in product selection, design, and engineering; however, this area is still in its infancy. The most successful production applications are using Big Data to improve infrastructure, monitor customer feedback through the Social Media Command Center, and advance micro-segmentation and intelligent campaigns.

We discussed the Advanced Analytics Platform (AAP) as the overall integrated architecture that combines Big Data with traditional Business Intelligence and Data Warehouse components. Most of the greenfield organizations are leapfrogging using Big Data Analytics and have taken a revolutionary approach to their analytics architecture. However, mature organizations with significant investment in BI and Data Warehousing are using more of an evolutionary approach to the overall architecture, with a hybrid architecture that combines the traditional data warehouse architecture with the newer Big Data capabilities.

We posed three questions at the beginning of this book. Let us try to answer them now using the material discussed in the book.

1. *What is Big Data and what are others doing with it?*
    Chapters 1 and 2 provided a definition of Big Data in terms of velocity, volume, variety, and veracity and discussed the popularity of Big Data due to market forces. The use cases provided examples of how businesses are using Big Data today.

2. *How do we build a strategic plan for Big Data Analytics in response to a management request?*
    Big Data Analytics is a multi-year, multi-phase journey. It is important to have a strategic vision that aligns with industry direction and responds well to the disruptive forces. It is also important to pick a target that makes a substantial impact on the organization. However, it is equally important to select short-term projects with short durations and measurable impact. Choosing areas closer to product engineering, operations, or infrastructure will provide quick and early results. Privacy is a difficult topic that should be handled with care.

3. *How does Big Data change our analytics organization and architecture?*
    The Big Data Analytics program does not work in a silo. Integration with the current environment is probably the most difficult part of the development activity. Care must be taken in establishing a strategic architecture along the lines discussed in Chapter 5 and in experimenting to see how an integrated architecture would support business processes using a combination of Big Data and conventional analytics tools.

Big Data is still an emerging topic. However, it has already resulted in major disruptions in many markets. In the world of analytics, it has changed how we view BI. Unlike in the past, where operational information was collected in the warehouse to be analyzed and researched over the long haul, current-day technologies are bringing analytics closer to the conversation. It requires the orchestration and conversation layers of the architecture in order to respond to the velocity and volume of data.

Notes

1. Sunil Soares, "A Framework That Focuses on the Data in Big Data Governance," *IBM Data Management*, June 13, 2012. *http://ibmdatamag.com/2012/06/a-framework-that-focuses-on-the-data-in-big-data-governance*.

2. "What Data Says About Us," *Fortune*, September 24, 2012, p. 163.

3. "Top 10 Largest Databases in the World," March 17, 2010. *http://www.comparebusinessproducts.com/fyi/10-largest-databases-in-the-world*.

4. "Statshot: How Mobile Data Traffic Will Grow by 2016," August 23, 2012. *http://gigaom.com/mobile/global-mobile-data-forecast*.

5. Kate Maddox, "Turn Ad Inspired by 'Mad Men'," *www.btobonline.com*, July 16, 2012.

6. Ben Grubb, "Can't Buy Love Online? 'Likes' for Sale," *www.stuff.co.nz*, August 24, 2012.

7. Rob Van Den Dam, *Global Telecom Consumer Survey*, IBM Institute for Business Value, 2011.

8. Ibid.

9. *http://www.iab.net/about_the_iab/recent_press_releases/press_release_archive/press_release/pr-041311*.

10. *http://www.yelp.com*.

11. Amir Efrati, "Online Ads: Where 1,240 Companies Fit In," *Wall Street Journal*, June 6, 2011.

12. Valerie Bauerlein, "Gatorade's 'Mission': Sell More Drinks," *Wall Street Journal*, September 13, 2010. Adam, Ostrow, "Inside Gatorade's Social Media Command Center," Mashable Social Media, June 15, 2010. Also see the YouTube video at *http://www.youtube.com/watch?v=InrOvEE2v38*.

13. Jeff Bertolucci, "Smart Phones, Big Data Help Fix Boston's Potholes," *Information Week*, July 25, 2012.

14. "Predictive Analytics: Police Use Analytics to Reduce Crime," *http://www.youtube.com/watch?v=_ZyU6po_E74&feature=relmfu*.

15. By "opting-in," a consumer may choose to allow use of location information, typically in exchange for a free or discounted service.

16. Don Peppers and Martha Rogers, *The One to One Future: Building Relationships One Customer at a Time*, Bantam Press, 1997.

17. Robert Lee Hotz, "The Really Smart Phone." *Wall Street Journal*, April 23, 2011.

18. Robert Andrews, "NBC: Nearly Half of Olympic Streams are from Mobile, Tablet." August 2, 2012, Paid Content, *www.paidcontent.org.*

19. Kuang-Chih Lee, Burkay Orten, Ali Dasdan, Wentong Li, "Estimating Conversion Rate in Display Advertising from Past Performance Data." *www.turn.com.*

20. Tom White, *Hadoop: the Definitive Guide,* O'Reilly Yahoo! Press, 2009.

21. T.R. Gruber, "A Translation Approach to Portable Ontologies," *Knowledge Acquisition* 5, no. 2 (1993): 199–220, 1993. Also see A. Sathi, M. Fox, and M. Greenberg, "Representation of Activity Knowledge for Project Management," *IEEE Transactions on Pattern Analysis and Machine Intelligence* 7, no. 5 (May 1985).

22. Jeff Hefflin, "OWL Web Ontology Language: Use Cases and Requirements," *www.w3.org.*

23. John Dawes, "Close the Multi-Channel Customer Experience Gap," *www.tealeaf.com,* January 2011.

24. Drew Fitzgerald, "Yahoo Passwords Stolen in Latest Data Breach," *Wall Street Journal,* July 12, 2012.

25. Charles Duhigg, "How Companies Learn Your Secrets," *New York Times,* February 16, 2012.

26. Anick Jesdanun, "FTC Finalizes Privacy Settlement with Facebook," *Huffington Post,* August 10, 2012.

27. Garland Grammer, Shallin Joshi, William Kroeschel, Arvind Sathi, Sudir Kumar, Mahesh Viswanathan, "Obfuscating Sensitive Data While Preserving Data Usability," USPTO Patent Number 20090132419. United States Patent and Trademark Office: *http://www.uspto.gov.*

28. William Kroeschel, Arvind Sathi, Mahesh Viswanathan, "Masking Related Sensitive Data in Groups," USPTO Patent Number 20090132575. United States Patent and Trademark Office: *http://www.uspto.gov.*

29. Julia Angwin, "A New Type of Tracking: Akamai's Pixel-Free Technology," *Wall Street Journal,* November 30, 2010. *http://blogs.wsj.com/digits/2010/11/30/a-new-type-of-tracking-akamais-pixel-free-technology.*

30. "The Best Performance Is the One You Can't See," IBM Website, *www-05.ibm.com/innovation/fr/rolandgarros/en.*

31. Brandon Gutman, "Fischer-Price on Connecting with Moms in the Digital World," *Forbes,* September 13, 2012.

Abbreviations

AAP	Advanced Analytics Platform
BI	Business Intelligence
BSS	Business Support System
CCI	Cognos Consumer Insight
CDR	Call Detail Record
CSP	Communications Service Provider
DMP	Data Management Platform
DSP	Demand Side Platform
DW	Data Warehouse
ETL	Extract Load Transform
HA	High Availability
HDFS	Hadoop Distributed File System
IPO	Initial Public Offering
IVR	Interactive Voice Response
KPI	Key Performance Indicator
MDM	Master Data Management
MPP	Massively Parallel Platform
NBA	Next Best Action
OLTP	On-Line Transaction Processing
OSS	Operations Support System
PII	Personally Identifiable Information
PoS	Point of Sale
SMP	Symmetric Multi-Processing
SSP	Supply Side Platform
STB	Set Top Box
STP	Straight Through Processing